MAGIC
TEA

A *Campbell* COOKBOOK

MOST-FOR-THE-MONEY

main dishes

Recipes Developed and Tested by
Home Economists of Campbell Kitchens

Photographer · G. William Holland

introduction

Most-for-the-money main dishes . . . tasty, satisfying, easily prepared. Dishes that are kind to your pocketbook. That's exactly what you'll find between these covers. The recipes call for on-hand ingredients and include canned Condensed Soups and Chunky Soups—those hard-working pantry staples which help make a little go a long way, deliciously.

Whether you use Campbell's Soups as an appetizer, a quick sauce, or an integral part of casseroles and stove-top dishes, they pay handsome dividends in time, energy, and quality.

And quality, flavor, and nutrition are important. The recipes in this book show how you can serve good food from skillet, oven, or saucepan—meal after imaginative meal. All this without breaking the bank.

Some of the recipes are meatless; some are designed for a crowd. There's even a section featuring everything *but* main dishes!

Whatever you choose to make, two things are certain: You'll enjoy serving the best for less, and everyone else will simply enjoy. Happy eating!

Front Cover Photo—Burgers 'n' Vegetables, recipe page 55

Back Cover Photo—Stuffed Shells Neapolitan, recipe page 72

1st Photo—Country Kitchen Casserole, recipe page 18

2nd Photo—Knockwurst and Cabbage, recipe page 10

table of contents

a primer on nutrition

Nutrition on a budget? You bet! It's one area where your knowledge counts more than what's in your wallet. Once you know which foods and how much of each your family needs every day, the choices are yours. Even the most expensive food item has a less costly cousin to provide needed nutrients. Broiled lobster may be your first love, yet an equal amount of canned tuna supplies the same high quality protein for dollars less—and it can be equally as tempting.

Here is a practical guide to good nutrition: The Four Food Groups.

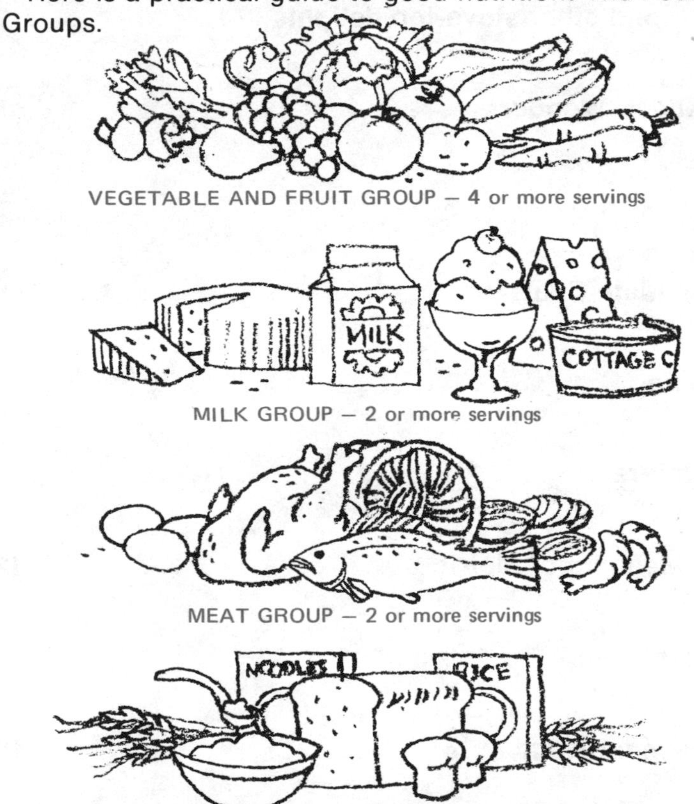

VEGETABLE AND FRUIT GROUP – 4 or more servings

MILK GROUP – 2 or more servings

MEAT GROUP – 2 or more servings

BREAD AND CEREAL GROUP – 4 or more servings

Simply keep track of the number of servings required from each group every day and plan your menus accordingly. Be sure to include everything—snacks and food eaten away from home, too.

Because foods from the Meat Group eat up the greatest part of your grocery dollar—and are the most important protein source—they almost always are featured in the main dish. So what better place to start a menu plan? Think of the entrée as the hub of the meal and let foods from the other groups—fruits, vegetables, breads, dairy products, "extras" . . . revolve around it.

Here are several menus. Use them as is or adjust them to fit your family's preferences, nutritional needs, and eating patterns.

"V-8" Cocktail Vegetable Juice
Stuffed Flounder Roll-ups
(page 61)
Fluffy Buttered Rice
Pepper Slaw
Baking-Powder Biscuits
Chocolate Cake
Coffee - Tea - Milk

Jumbo Tuna Gumbo
(page 99)
Hearts of Lettuce
with
Green Goddess Dressing
Hard Rolls
Cheesecake Pie
(page 110)

Oven Fried Chicken
Scalloped Potatoes
(page 104)
Molded Carrot &
Pineapple Salad
Brownie
Coffee - Tea - Milk

Tamale Pie
(page 11)
Tossed Salad with
Dressing
Mixed Fruit & Melon Cup
Coffee - Tea - Milk

When it comes time to select foods for other menus CONTRAST is the key to success. Balance Tomato-Mushroom Rabbit (page 73) with crisp salad greens. Accent mellow Chicken Zucchini Skillet (page 54) with tangy cranberry relish. Couple the vibrant colors of broccoli or tomatoes with the muted tones of Easy Oven Fillets (page 75).

In other words, make meals appetizing to the last forkful. Empty plates mean nutrients-at-work and money well-spent.

Here again, the budget takes a back seat to brainwork. With thoughtful planning and careful preparation, anyone can put together a million dollar meal at five and dime prices. The simplest, pennywise dishes are memorable when done to perfection and served with flair.

# of casseroles and compliments

Nothing compares to the mingling of hearty flavors in a piping hot casserole. So smile as you tuck one of the following dishes neatly into the oven. Your family will when they catch a whiff of that *"come and get it"* aroma. And again when they dig in. Cheers to the cook!

DEEP DISH TURKEY PIE

1 cup sliced celery
Generous dash onion powder
2 tablespoons butter or margarine
1 can (10¾ ounces) condensed cream of chicken soup
1½ cups cubed cooked turkey or chicken
1½ cups cooked carrots cut in 1-inch pieces
¼ cup milk
2 teaspoons lemon juice
⅛ teaspoon ground nutmeg
½ cup biscuit mix
2 tablespoons cold water

In saucepan, cook celery with onion in butter until tender. Stir in remaining ingredients except biscuit mix and water. Bring to boil; stir occasionally. Meanwhile, to make pastry, combine biscuit mix and water. Roll pastry to fit top of 1-quart casserole. Pour hot chicken mixture into casserole; top with pastry. Trim edges; make several slits in pastry. Bake at 450°F. for 15 minutes or until done. Makes about 3½ cups.

TUNA VERDÉ

2 packages (10 ounces each) frozen chopped spinach, cooked and drained
1 can (11 ounces) condensed Cheddar cheese soup
1 can (about 7 ounces) tuna, drained and flaked
2 hard-cooked eggs, chopped
½ cup chopped canned tomatoes
⅛ teaspoon oregano leaves, crushed
2 tablespoons buttered bread crumbs

Combine all ingredients except bread crumbs. Pour into 1½-quart shallow baking dish (10x6x2"). Bake at 450°F. for 20 minutes or until hot; stir. Top with crumbs; bake 5 minutes more. Makes about 4 cups.

FIRST THINGS FIRST: *You can prevent staples and canned goods from becoming has-beens by rotating them so that the oldest is always used first. Better yet, date packages at time of purchase.*

BEST EVER MEAT LOAF

1 can (10¾ ounces) condensed cream of mushroom or golden mushroom soup
2 pounds ground beef
½ cup fine dry bread crumbs
⅓ cup finely chopped onion
1 egg, slightly beaten
1 teaspoon salt
⅓ cup water

Mix *thoroughly* ½ cup soup, beef, bread crumbs, onion, egg, and salt. Shape *firmly* into loaf (8x4"); place in shallow baking pan. Bake at 375°F. for 1 hour 15 minutes. Blend remaining soup, water, and 2 to 3 tablespoons drippings. Heat; stir occasionally. Serve with loaf. Makes 6 servings.

Frosted Meat Loaf: Prepare loaf as above; bake for 1 hour. Frost loaf with 4 cups mashed potatoes; sprinkle with shredded Cheddar cheese. Bake 15 minutes more. Serve with sauce.

Swedish Meat Loaf: Add ½ teaspoon nutmeg to loaf. Blend remaining soup with ⅓ cup sour cream; omit drippings and water. Serve over loaf; sprinkle with additional nutmeg. Garnish with thinly sliced cucumber.

Meat Loaf Wellington:
Crescent Rolls *(Refrigerated):* Prepare loaf as above. Bake at 375°F. for 1 hour. Spoon off fat. Separate 1 package (8 ounces) refrigerated crescent dinner rolls; place crosswise over top and down sides of meat loaf, overlapping slightly. Bake 15 minutes more. Serve with sauce.
Patty Shells: Thaw 1 package (10 ounces) frozen puff pastry patty shells. Prepare loaf as above. Bake at 375°F. for 30 minutes. Spoon off fat. Increase oven temperature to 400°F. On floured board, roll 5 patty shells into rectangle (12x8"); prick several times with fork. Cover top and sides of loaf with pastry. Decorate top with remaining patty shell, rolled and cut into fancy shapes. Bake for 45 minutes more or until golden brown. Serve with sauce.

UPSIDE-DOWN MEAT PIE

1 pound ground beef
½ cup chopped celery
½ cup chopped onion
¼ cup chopped green pepper
1 can (10¾ ounces) condensed tomato soup
1 teaspoon prepared mustard
1½ cups biscuit mix
⅓ cup cold water
3 slices (about 3 ounces) process cheese, cut in half diagonally

In 10" oven-proof skillet, brown beef and cook celery, onion, and green pepper until tender (use shortening if necessary). Stir to separate meat; *drain well*. Stir in soup and mustard. Combine biscuit mix and water; roll or pat dough into a circle slightly smaller than skillet. Spread meat mixture evenly in skillet; top with biscuit dough. Bake at 450°F. for 15 minutes or until browned. Turn upside down on platter. Top with cheese. Cut in wedges and serve. Makes 6 servings.

BAKED CHICKEN WITH NOODLES

2 pounds chicken parts
1 tablespoon melted butter or margarine
1 can (10¾ ounces) condensed chicken broth
½ cup water
2 teaspoons Italian salad dressing mix
1 teaspoon sesame seed
3 cups uncooked medium noodles
1 package (9 ounces) frozen cut green beans
Paprika

In 2-quart shallow baking dish (12x8x2"), arrange chicken skin-side down. Pour butter over. Bake at 400°F. for 20 minutes; remove chicken. Stir in remaining ingredients except paprika. Arrange chicken skin-side up on noodle mixture; sprinkle with paprika. Bake covered 40 minutes more or until done. Stir noodle mixture before serving. Makes 4 servings.

***OUT OF THE APPLE BARREL** . . . into the refrigerator. Apples are less likely to deteriorate when stored in the refrigerator. Following harvest in the fall they may be kept in any cool place (below 60°F.).*

BURGER-RICE BAKE

- 2 cans (19 ounces each) chunky sirloin burger soup
- 1 cup quick-cooking rice, uncooked
- 1 cup stewed tomatoes
- 2 teaspoons chili powder

In 1½-quart shallow baking dish (10x6x2″), combine ingredients. Bake at 400°F. for 25 minutes or until rice is done; stir. Garnish with sliced hard-cooked egg if desired. Makes about 5 cups.

KNOCKWURST AND CABBAGE

- 1 small head cabbage (about 1 pound), cut in 4 wedges
- 1 can (10¾ ounces) condensed cream of celery soup
- ¼ cup milk
- 1 cup chopped apple
- ½ teaspoon caraway seed
- 1 pound knockwurst (4 links), slashed

In saucepan, cook cabbage in boiling water 10 minutes; drain. In 1½-quart shallow baking dish (10x6x2″), arrange cabbage. Combine soup, milk, apple, and caraway; pour over cabbage. Arrange knockwurst between cabbage wedges. Bake at 400°F. for 25 minutes or until hot. Stir sauce before serving. Makes 4 servings.

WAGONWHEEL TUNA BAKE

- 1 can (10¾ ounces) condensed cream of mushroom soup
- 2 cups cooked rice
- ⅓ cup milk
- 1 tablespoon lemon juice
- 2 cans (about 7 ounces each) tuna, drained and flaked
- 1 package (10 ounces) frozen broccoli spears, cooked and drained
- ½ cup shredded process cheese

In 9″ round baking dish, combine soup, rice, milk, lemon, and tuna. Bake at 400°F. for 20 minutes; stir. Arrange broccoli in spoke-fashion on top of rice mixture; sprinkle with cheese. Bake 10 minutes more or until hot. Makes 4 servings.

TAMALE PIE

1 pound ground beef
½ cup chopped onion
⅓ cup chopped green pepper
1 tablespoon salad oil
1 can (11¼ ounces) condensed chili beef soup
1 can (16 ounces) tomatoes
⅓ cup sliced ripe olives
1 to 2 tablespoons chili powder
1 large clove garlic, minced
3 cups water
1 cup corn meal
½ teaspoon salt
1 cup shredded Cheddar cheese

In skillet, brown beef and cook onion and green pepper in oil until tender. Stir to separate meat; pour off fat. Stir in soup, tomatoes, olives, chili powder, and garlic. Cook over low heat 15 minutes; stir occasionally. Meanwhile, bring 2 cups water to boil. Mix corn meal with salt and 1 cup cold water; pour into boiling water, stirring constantly. Cook over medium heat until thickened (about 15 minutes); stir occasionally. Line bottom and sides of buttered 2-quart shallow baking dish (12x8x2") with cooked corn meal. Fill with chili mixture; bake at 350°F. for 30 minutes. Top with cheese; bake until cheese melts. Makes 6 servings.

PIZZA STRATA

10 slices white bread, cut in 1-inch cubes (about 7 cups)
2 cups shredded sharp Cheddar cheese
1 can (10¾ ounces) condensed tomato soup
1 soup can water
4 eggs, slightly beaten
1 teaspoon oregano leaves, crushed

In buttered 2-quart shallow baking dish (12x8x2"), arrange bread cubes; top with cheese. In bowl, combine remaining ingredients; pour over bread. Cover; refrigerate overnight. Uncover; bake at 350°F. for 30 minutes or until set. Makes 6 servings.

ONE POTATO, TWO POTATO: Pound for pound, all-purpose potatoes are usually less expensive than baking potatoes. Use them for everything—including baking.

MEAT 'n' VEGETABLE BAKE

1 can (10¾ ounces) condensed cream of celery soup
⅓ cup milk
2 tablespoons chopped parsley
1 tablespoon pickle relish
½ teaspoon prepared mustard
1 can (12 ounces) luncheon meat, cubed
1 package (10 ounces) frozen cauliflower, cooked and drained
1 package (10 ounces) frozen mixed vegetables, cooked and drained
¼ cup buttered bread crumbs

In 1½-quart casserole combine all ingredients except bread crumbs. Bake at 350°F. for 25 minutes or until hot; stir. Sprinkle with bread crumbs. Bake 5 minutes more. Makes about 5 cups.

CHILI FRANK ROUNDUP

½ pound frankfurters, cut in 1-inch pieces
1 cup chopped onion
2 tablespoons butter or margarine
1 can (11¼ ounces) condensed chili beef soup
½ cup water
¼ cup prepared barbecue sauce
1 can (about 8 ounces) whole kernel corn, drained
2 cups cooked elbow macaroni
2 slices (about 2 ounces) process cheese, cut in 8 strips

In saucepan, brown frankfurters and cook onion in butter until tender. Stir in remaining ingredients except cheese. Pour into 1½-quart casserole. Bake at 400°F. for 25 minutes or until hot; stir. Arrange cheese in lattice shape on top of casserole. Bake until cheese melts. Makes about 5½ cups.

TACO CHICKEN

- 1 can (10¾ ounces) condensed cream of chicken soup
- ⅓ cup chili sauce
- ⅓ cup water
- ¼ teaspoon hot pepper sauce
- 3 whole chicken breasts (about 2 pounds), split
- ⅓ cup flour
- 3 cups finely crushed taco-flavored corn chips (about 10 ounces)
- 2 tablespoons melted butter or margarine

Mix soup, chili sauce, water, and hot pepper sauce. Dust chicken with flour; dip in soup mixture. Roll in chips. Place on rack in shallow baking pan. Drizzle with butter. Bake at 400°F. for 1 hour or until done. Makes 4 servings.

SOUTHWEST FRANKFURTERS

- ½ cup chopped onion
- 2 tablespoons butter or margarine
- 1 can (10¾ ounces) condensed tomato soup
- ⅓ cup water
- 1½ cups cooked spiral-shaped macaroni
- 1 can (about 8 ounces) vacuum packed whole kernel corn, undrained
- 1 tablespoon sweet pickle relish
- 1 teaspoon prepared mustard
- ½ pound frankfurters, slashed

In saucepan, cook onion in butter until tender. Stir in remaining ingredients except frankfurters. Pour into 1½-quart shallow baking dish (10x6x2"); top with frankfurters. Bake at 400°F. for 20 minutes or until hot. Makes 4 servings.

IF THE QUALITY FITS, BUY IT: *Grades are one indication of food quality. Lower grades are as nutritious as higher grades, but are often less visually attractive or uniform in size, and should cost less. The end use tells the story.*

CHEESE 'n' NOODLE BAKE

1 can (10¾ ounces) condensed cream of mushroom soup
¼ cup milk
½ cup drained chopped canned tomatoes
¼ teaspoon oregano leaves, crushed
Generous dash garlic salt
1½ cups shredded process cheese
3 cups cooked large bow noodles
Grated Parmesan cheese

In 1½-quart casserole, blend soup, milk, tomatoes, oregano, and garlic salt. Stir in process cheese and noodles. Bake at 400°F. for 25 minutes or until hot; stir. Garnish with Parmesan cheese. Makes about 4½ cups.

HAMBURGER NOODLE STROGANOFF

1 pound ground beef
½ cup chopped onion
1 can (10¾ ounces) condensed cream of mushroom soup
½ cup sour cream
½ cup water
½ teaspoon paprika
½ teaspoon salt
⅛ teaspoon pepper
2 cups cooked noodles

In skillet, brown beef and cook onion until tender (use shortening if necessary). Stir to separate meat; pour off fat. Add remaining ingredients. Pour into 1½-quart shallow baking dish (10x6x2"). Bake at 400°F. for 25 minutes or until hot; stir. Garnish with tomato slices and buttered bread crumbs the last 5 minutes of baking if desired. Makes about 4½ cups.

CHICKEN PIE AU GRATIN

1 can (19 ounces) chunky chicken soup
1 package (10 ounces) frozen peas & carrots, cooked and drained
1 cup shredded Cheddar cheese
⅛ teaspoon rubbed sage
Pastry for 1-crust pie

In 2-quart shallow baking dish (12x8x2"), combine soup, peas & carrots, cheese, and sage. Roll pastry to fit top of dish; place on soup mixture. Trim edges. Sprinkle with paprika if desired. Make several slits in pastry. Bake at 400°F. for 35 minutes or until done. Makes about 3½ cups.

TWO-WAY CASSEROLE

½ cup chopped onion
2 tablespoons butter or margarine
1 can (10¾ ounces) condensed cream of chicken soup
1 can (10¾ ounces) condensed cream of mushroom soup
⅔ cup milk
½ teaspoon salt
⅛ teaspoon pepper
3 cups cubed cooked chicken or ham
4 cups cooked noodles
½ cup shredded Cheddar cheese

In saucepan, cook onion in butter until tender; add remaining ingredients except cheese. Pour into 2-quart shallow baking dish (12x8x2"). Bake at 400°F. for 25 minutes or until hot; stir. Top with cheese. Bake until cheese melts. Makes about 7 cups.

PEANUT BUTTER-JELLY STRATA

12 slices white bread
¾ cup chunk-style peanut butter
½ cup grape jelly
1 can (10¾ ounces) condensed cream of chicken soup
1 soup can milk
4 eggs, slightly beaten
Cinnamon
Maple-flavored syrup

Make 6 peanut butter and jelly sandwiches; cut in half diagonally. In 2½-quart shallow baking dish (13x9x2"), arrange sandwich halves overlapping slightly. In bowl, combine soup, milk, and eggs; pour over sandwiches. Sprinkle with cinnamon. Cover; refrigerate 1 hour. Uncover; bake at 350°F. for 30 minutes or until set. Serve with syrup. Makes 6 servings.

HAM SLICE FLORENTINE

1 can (10¾ ounces) condensed cream of mushroom soup
¼ cup milk
1 package (10 ounces) frozen chopped spinach, cooked and well-drained
2 tablespoons chopped pimiento
⅛ teaspoon rosemary leaves, crushed
1 pound ham slice (¾-inch thick), cut into 4 pieces
¼ cup herb seasoned stuffing mix

In 1½-quart shallow baking dish (10x6x2"), combine soup, milk, spinach, pimiento, and rosemary. Top with ham; sprinkle with stuffing mix. Bake at 450°F. for 20 minutes or until hot. Makes 4 servings.

HOT DOG! POTATO BAKE

1 can (10¾ ounces) condensed cream of celery soup
½ cup milk
1 to 2 tablespoons dried parsley flakes
1 tablespoon prepared mustard
2 cans (about 16 ounces each) small whole white potatoes, drained and sliced
1 pound frankfurters, cut in 1-inch pieces

In 2-quart casserole, combine soup, milk, parsley, and mustard; stir in potatoes and frankfurters. Bake at 400°F. for 30 minutes or until hot; stir. Makes about 6 cups.

BAKED MACARONI 'n' CHEESE

1 can (10¾ ounces) condensed cream of mushroom soup
½ cup milk
½ teaspoon prepared mustard
Generous dash pepper
3 cups cooked elbow macaroni
2 cups shredded Cheddar cheese
1 cup French fried onions

In 1½-quart casserole, blend soup, milk, mustard, and pepper. Stir in macaroni and 1½ cups cheese. Bake at 400°F. for 25 minutes or until hot; stir. Top with onions and remaining cheese; bake 5 minutes more or until cheese melts. Makes about 4½ cups.

THE BIG CHEESE: *When cheese is already grated, shredded, or sliced, you pay extra for handling and packaging. Buy whole pieces and save.*

PORK CHOPS VIA VENETO

6 pork chops (about 1½ pounds)
Salt
Pepper
1 can (10¾ ounces) condensed tomato soup
⅓ cup water
3 cups cooked elbow macaroni
1 cup shredded mild process cheese
⅓ cup finely chopped green pepper
¼ cup finely chopped onion
2 teaspoons Worcestershire
1 teaspoon prepared mustard
Dash hot pepper sauce

In skillet, brown chops (use shortening if necessary); pour off fat. Season with salt and pepper; remove chops from skillet. Add remaining ingredients. Heat until cheese melts. Pour into 2-quart shallow baking dish (12x8x2"); top with chops. Cover; bake at 350°F. for 15 minutes. Uncover; bake 15 minutes more or until done. Makes 4 servings.

PARMESAN CHICKEN

¼ cup fine dry bread crumbs
4 tablespoons grated Parmesan cheese
¼ teaspoon oregano leaves, crushed
Dash garlic powder
Dash pepper
2 pounds chicken parts
1 can (10¾ ounces) condensed cream of mushroom soup
½ cup milk
Paprika

Combine crumbs, 2 tablespoons Parmesan, oregano, garlic, and pepper; roll chicken in mixture. Arrange in 2-quart shallow baking dish (12x8x2"). Bake at 400°F. for 20 minutes. Turn chicken; bake 20 minutes more. Meanwhile, blend soup and milk; pour over chicken. Sprinkle with paprika and remaining Parmesan. Bake 20 minutes more or until done. Arrange chicken on platter. Stir sauce; pour over chicken. Makes 4 servings.

COUNTRY KITCHEN CASSEROLE

1 can (10¾ ounces) condensed cream of mushroom soup
¼ cup water
2 teaspoons prepared mustard
1 teaspoon Worcestershire
1 cup shredded Cheddar cheese
2 cans (about 16 ounces each) small whole white potatoes, drained and sliced
1 package (10 ounces) frozen peas, cooked and drained
1 can (12 ounces) luncheon meat, cut in 6 slices

In bowl, combine soup, water, mustard, Worcestershire, and cheese; add potatoes and peas. Spoon into 1½-quart shallow baking dish (10x6x2"); top with meat. Bake at 400°F. for 25 minutes or until hot. Makes 6 servings.

PORK CHOP 'n' POTATO SCALLOP

4 pork chops (about 1 pound)
Salt
Pepper
1 can (10¾ ounces) condensed cream of mushroom soup
½ cup sour cream
¼ cup water
½ teaspoon dried dill weed, crushed
4 cups thinly sliced potatoes
Parsley

In skillet, brown chops (use shortening if necessary); season with salt and pepper. Blend soup, sour cream, water, and dill. In 2-quart casserole, alternate layers of potatoes and sauce; cover. Bake at 375°F. for 45 minutes. Top with chops. Cover; bake 30 minutes more or until done. Garnish with parsley. Makes 3 servings.

NO-FROST AT LESS COST: *If you have a self-defrosting refrigerator, check the condensate drain every so often to make sure it's clean. A prolonged blockage will cause ice to build up on the coils, making the unit inefficient.*

Clean the condenser coils in the back of the unit, too. In newer refrigerators, the coils are beneath the unit. To clean, remove the front grill and vacuum.

TUNA PUFF

- 1 can (10¾ ounces) condensed cream of mushroom soup
- ⅓ cup milk
- 2 cups cooked rice
- 1 package (10 ounces) chopped broccoli, cooked and drained
- 2 cans (about 7 ounces each) tuna, drained and flaked
- ⅛ teaspoon ground nutmeg
- 4 eggs, separated
- 1 tablespoon grated Parmesan cheese

In 1½-quart shallow baking dish (10x6x2"), combine soup, milk, rice, broccoli, tuna, and nutmeg. Bake at 400°F. for 20 minutes. Meanwhile, beat egg yolks until thick and lemon-colored; add cheese. Using clean egg beater, beat egg whites until soft peaks form; fold in egg yolk mixture. Remove casserole from oven; stir. Gently spread egg mixture over top. Bake 15 minutes more or until golden brown. Makes about 5 cups.

HAM SPOONBREAD

- 1 cup finely chopped ham
- ¼ cup finely chopped onion
- 2 tablespoons butter or margarine
- 1 can (10¾ ounces) condensed cream of mushroom soup
- ½ soup can milk
- Dash cayenne pepper
- ½ cup corn meal
- 3 eggs, separated
- Syrup or butter

In saucepan, brown ham and cook onion in butter until tender. Stir in soup, milk, and cayenne. Add corn meal. Bring to boil; reduce heat. Cook until thickened, stirring. Remove from heat. Beat egg yolks until thick and lemon-colored; stir into corn meal mixture. Using clean egg beater, beat egg whites until stiff but not dry. Gradually fold into corn meal mixture. Pour into buttered 1½-quart casserole. Bake at 350°F. for 1 hour. Serve with syrup. Makes 4 servings.

SHEPHERD'S PIE

- ¼ cup finely chopped onion
- Generous dash crushed thyme leaves
- 2 tablespoons butter or margarine
- 1 can (10¾ ounces) condensed golden mushroom soup
- ¼ cup water
- 1½ cups cubed cooked beef
- 1 package (10 ounces) frozen peas and carrots, cooked and drained
- 4 servings prepared instant mashed potatoes

In saucepan, cook onion with thyme in butter until tender; add remaining ingredients except potatoes. Pour into 1½-quart casserole. Spoon potatoes around edge of casserole. Bake at 400°F. for 30 minutes or until hot. Makes about 3½ cups.

MEXICALI PIE

- 1 pound frankfurters, cut in 1-inch pieces
- 1 cup chopped onion
- 2 tablespoons butter or margarine
- 1 can (10¾ ounces) condensed tomato soup
- 1 can (11¼ ounces) condensed chili beef soup
- 1 package (9 ounces) frozen cut green beans, cooked and drained
- ¼ cup water
- ½ package (12 to 14-ounce size) corn muffin mix (about 1 cup)
- ⅓ cup milk
- 1 egg

In skillet, brown frankfurters and cook onion in butter until tender. Add soups, beans, and water; bring to boil. Pour into 2-quart shallow baking dish (12x8x2"). Combine corn muffin mix, milk, and egg. Spoon evenly around edge of baking dish. Bake at 400°F. for 20 minutes or until done. Makes about 5½ cups.

BEYOND A LICK AND A PROMISE: *Here's just the incentive you've been needing to clean that oven and broiler: When free of grease and grime, these appliances cook more efficiently, save gas and electricity.*

MEAT-SHELL POTATO PIE

- 1 can (10¾ ounces) condensed cream of mushroom soup
- 1 pound ground beef
- ¼ cup finely chopped onion
- 1 egg, slightly beaten
- ¼ cup fine dry bread crumbs
- 2 tablespoons chopped parsley
- ¼ teaspoon salt
- Dash pepper
- 2 cups mashed potatoes
- ¼ cup shredded mild cheese
- Cooked bacon, crumbled

Mix *thoroughly* ½ cup soup, beef, onion, egg, bread crumbs, parsley, and seasonings. Press *firmly* into 9-inch pie plate. Bake at 350°F. for 25 minutes; spoon off fat. Frost with potatoes; top with remaining soup, cheese, and bacon. Bake 10 minutes more or until done. Makes one 9-inch meat pie.

TUNA POTATO BAKE

- 1 can (10¾ ounces) condensed cream of celery soup
- ⅓ cup water
- ¼ cup mayonnaise
- 2 tablespoons chopped parsley
- 1 teaspoon lemon juice
- ⅛ teaspoon dry mustard
- 4 cups cubed cooked potatoes
- 2 cans (about 7 ounces each) tuna, drained and flaked
- 3 slices (about 3 ounces) mild process cheese, cut in half diagonally

In 2-quart casserole, blend soup, water, mayonnaise, parsley, lemon juice, and mustard. Stir in potatoes and tuna. Bake at 400°F. for 30 minutes or until hot; stir. Top with cheese. Bake 5 minutes more or until cheese melts. Makes about 6 cups.

ADVANCED DEGREES: *How do you know when your oven is pre-heated? An oven thermometer tells you exactly. Otherwise, wait about 10 minutes. Most important: avoid pre-heating longer than necessary at a higher setting than called for. Dialing higher will not heat the oven faster. What's more, you just might forget to turn the setting back.*

stout-hearted skilletry

And Other Stove-Top Delights

Take one sturdy skillet, add the ingredients in the following recipes, and relax—some stick-to-the-ribs eating is on the way. Rustle up these robust dishes whenever you need something quick-to-fix and sure-to-please. Easy does it.

ALPINE MEATBALLS

½ pound ground beef
2 tablespoons fine dry bread crumbs
2 tablespoons finely chopped onion
¼ teaspoon salt
1 egg, slightly beaten
2 tablespoons shortening
1 can (10¾ ounces) condensed cream of mushroom soup
¼ cup water
¼ cup chopped canned tomatoes
2 tablespoons chopped parsley
¼ teaspoon basil leaves, crushed
2 cups cooked noodles
⅓ cup grated Parmesan cheese

In bowl, mix *thoroughly* beef, crumbs, onion, salt, and egg. Shape into 12 meatballs. In skillet, brown meatballs in shortening; pour off fat. Add soup, water, tomatoes, parsley, and basil. Cover; cook over low heat 20 minutes. Add noodles and cheese. Heat; stir occasionally. Makes about 4 cups.

ALL ABOARD! *Schedule your dishwasher for full loads only—once a day, if possible. Several meals-worth of dishes will make this appliance run farther on less—energy, detergent, water.*

BOLOGNA RICE COMBO

2 cups cubed bologna
¾ cup raw regular rice
1 cup sliced celery
2 tablespoons butter or margarine
1 can (10½ ounces) condensed onion soup
1 soup can water

In skillet, brown bologna and rice and cook celery in butter until tender. Stir in soup and water; bring to boil. Reduce heat; cover. Cook over low heat 25 minutes or until rice is done. Stir occasionally. Makes about 4½ cups.

SASSY BEEF AND NOODLES

1 pound ground beef
1 medium onion, chopped
1 can (10¾ ounces) condensed cream of mushroom soup
¼ teaspoon hot pepper sauce
1 teaspoon salt
1 can (10½ ounces) condensed beef broth
1 cup water
3 cups uncooked medium noodles

In skillet, brown beef and cook onion until tender (use shortening if necessary). Stir to separate meat; pour off fat. Blend in mushroom soup, hot pepper sauce, and salt. Add remaining ingredients. Bring to boil; reduce heat. Cover; cook 10 minutes or until noodles are done. Stir often. Makes about 5 cups.

STUFFED CHICKEN ROLL-UPS

3 chicken breasts, split, skinned, and boned (about 1½ pounds boneless)
1 can (10¾ ounces) condensed cream of onion soup
1 cup small bread cubes
2 tablespoons chopped parsley
½ teaspoon oregano leaves, crushed
1 can (about 4 ounces) sliced mushrooms, drained
2 tablespoons butter or margarine
¼ cup water

Flatten chicken breasts with flat side of knife. To make stuffing, combine 3 tablespoons soup, bread cubes, parsley, and oregano. Place stuffing in center of each chicken breast. Roll up; tuck in ends. Secure with toothpicks. In skillet, brown chicken and mushrooms in butter. Add remaining soup and water. Cover; cook over low heat 20 minutes or until done. Stir occasionally. Makes 6 servings.

HAM AND TURKEY POLYNESIAN

½ cup diced cooked ham
½ cup green pepper strips
2 tablespoons butter or margarine
1 can (18¾ ounces) chunky turkey soup
¼ cup drained pineapple tidbits
¼ cup sliced water chestnuts
Dash salt
1 tablespoon cornstarch
2 tablespoons water
Cooked rice

In saucepan, brown ham and cook green pepper in butter until tender. Add soup, pineapple, water chestnuts, and salt. Blend cornstarch and water until smooth; add to soup mixture. Cook, stirring until thickened. Serve over rice. Makes about 3 cups.

SHOPPERS' ENEMY #1: *Impulse buying. This scoundrel takes control of your arm and is extremely dangerous to your budget. To protect yourself, carry a shopping list at all times, eat before you shop, and leave the rest of the family at home (especially if they are the* I want it *types).*

SKILLET CHICKEN BARBECUE

2 pounds chicken parts
2 tablespoons shortening
1 can (11 ounces) condensed tomato bisque soup
¼ cup chopped onion
2 teaspoons Worcestershire
½ teaspoon vinegar
Dash hot pepper sauce
1 package (9 ounces) frozen cut green beans

In skillet, brown chicken in shortening; pour off fat. Stir in remaining ingredients except beans. Cover; cook over low heat 30 minutes. Add beans. Cook 15 minutes more or until done. Stir occasionally. Makes 4 servings.

SKILLET STEAKS CASINO

1 pound boneless round steak (½-inch thick)
2 tablespoons shortening
1 can (10¾ ounces) condensed cream of onion soup
¾ cup water
¼ cup chili sauce
3 medium potatoes (about 1 pound), quartered
1 package (9 ounces) frozen cut green beans

Pound steak; cut into serving-size pieces. In skillet, brown steak in shortening; pour off fat. Add soup, water, and chili sauce. Cover; cook over low heat 30 minutes. Add potatoes; cook 45 minutes more. Add beans. Cook 20 minutes more or until done; stir occasionally. Makes 4 servings.

DENIZENS OF THE DEEP FREEZE: *Wouldn't it be nice to know exactly* who's who *in your freezer without benefit of X-ray eyes? Easy. Mark all packages with tape and waxed pencil before freezing. Keep an up-to-date inventory sheet near the freezer that tells the location of every item. Soon you'll be wisking food out with such speed that warm air won't have a chance to get inside and run up operating costs.*

COWPOKE CASSOULET

1 pound ground beef
1 medium onion, chopped
1 can (11¼ ounces) condensed chili beef soup
1 can (16 ounces) pork & beans with tomato sauce
¼ cup water

In skillet, brown beef and cook onion until tender (use shortening if necessary). Stir to separate meat; pour off fat. Add remaining ingredients. Heat; stir occasionally. Makes about 4½ cups.

MEATBALLS LA SCALA

½ pound ground beef
¼ teaspoon salt
Dash pepper
2 tablespoons shortening
1 can (19 ounces) chunky vegetable soup
½ cup uncooked thin spaghetti broken in pieces
1 small clove garlic, minced
¼ teaspoon Italian seasoning, crushed

Mix *thoroughly* beef, salt, and pepper. Shape into 16 meatballs. In saucepan, brown meatballs in shortening; pour off fat. Add remaining ingredients. Bring to boil; reduce heat. Cover; simmer 20 minutes or until done. Stir often. Makes about 3 cups.

SAUCY LIVER STRIPS

1 pound sliced beef liver, cut in strips
1 large clove garlic, minced
½ teaspoon oregano leaves, crushed
2 tablespoons butter or margarine
1 can (10¾ ounces) condensed tomato soup
¼ cup water
Cooked rice

In skillet, brown liver with garlic and oregano in butter. Add remaining ingredients except rice. Cover; cook over low heat 20 minutes or until done. Stir occasionally. Serve over rice. Makes about 2½ cups.

GOING BANANAS: *No need to let bananas get over-ripe and go uneaten. Ripen them to desired maturity at room temperature, then refrigerate until ready to use.*

If you do have over-ripe bananas on hand, that's the day to bake a banana quick-bread or cake—to eat, freeze, or give to a friend.

KLONDIKE CHICKEN

3-pound stewing chicken, cut up
Salt
Pepper
½ teaspoon paprika
2 tablespoons bacon drippings
2 medium green peppers, chopped
2 medium onions, chopped
1 can (10¾ ounces) condensed tomato soup
½ soup can water
1 cup diced cooked ham, sausage, or pork
¼ to ½ teaspoon red pepper flakes
½ teaspoon salt
Cooked rice

Season chicken with salt, pepper, and paprika. In large heavy pan, slowly brown chicken in bacon drippings (about 20 minutes); remove. Add green pepper and onion; cook until tender. Return chicken to pan; add remaining ingredients except rice. Cover; cook over low heat 35 minutes or until done. Stir occasionally. Skim excess fat from sauce; thicken if desired. Serve with rice. Makes 4 servings.

SPEEDY STROGANOFF

1 can (about 2 ounces) sliced mushrooms, drained
¼ cup chopped onion
2 tablespoons butter or margarine
1 can (19 ounces) chunky beef soup
¼ cup sour cream
1 cup cooked noodles
2 teaspoons paprika

In saucepan, brown mushrooms and cook onion in butter until tender. Add remaining ingredients. Heat; stir occasionally. Makes about 3 cups.

SAVORY STEW with DUMPLINGS

½ pound bulk sausage
2 cans (18¾ ounces each) chunky turkey soup
1 can (about 8 ounces) whole kernel corn, drained
⅛ teaspoon poultry seasoning
1 cup biscuit mix
⅓ cup milk
2 tablespoons chopped parsley

In saucepan, brown sausage; stir to separate meat. Pour off fat. Add soup, corn, and poultry seasoning. Bring to boil; stir occasionally. Meanwhile, combine biscuit mix, milk, and parsley. Drop 5 to 6 spoonfuls on boiling soup. Reduce heat; cook uncovered over low heat 10 minutes. Cover; cook 10 minutes more. Makes about 3½ cups.

JACK SPRAT DIDN'T KNOW WHAT HE WAS MISSING: *Improve the flavor of your cooking and save money doing it. How? Collect beef and bacon fats in small jars, adding more as you go along. Store in refrigerator. Use them for sautéeing potatoes, onions, and vegetables; for browning stew meat; and for frying chicken.*

DUTCH TREAT DINNER

2 frankfurters, sliced
¼ cup chopped onion
2 tablespoons butter or margarine
1 can (19 ounces) chunky split pea with ham soup
1 cup cooked elbow macaroni
2 tablespoons ketchup

In saucepan, brown frankfurters and cook onion in butter until tender. Add remaining ingredients. Heat; stir occasionally. Makes about 3 cups.

BURGERS ROMANESQUE

1 can (10¾ ounces) condensed cream of mushroom soup
1 pound ground beef
¼ cup fine dry bread crumbs
1 egg, slightly beaten
½ teaspoon salt
Generous dash pepper
2 cups sliced zucchini
½ cup sliced onion
½ cup drained chopped canned tomatoes
¼ teaspoon Italian seasoning, crushed
Dash garlic powder

Mix *thoroughly* ¼ cup soup, beef, bread crumbs, egg, salt, and pepper. Shape *firmly* into 4 patties. In skillet, brown patties (use shortening if necessary); pour off fat. Add remaining ingredients. Cover; cook over low heat 20 minutes or until done. Stir occasionally. Makes 4 servings.

CHICKEN ORIENT

1 pound fresh broccoli
2 tablespoons salad or peanut oil
2 whole chicken breasts (about 1½ pounds), split, skinned, boned, and cut in strips
¼ pound sliced fresh mushrooms (about 1 cup)
1 can (10¾ ounces) condensed cream of chicken soup
½ cup coarsely chopped cashews or peanuts
½ cup water
¼ cup chopped pimiento

Remove flowerets from broccoli; break into small pieces. Peel stalk and cut into thin strips (1-inch long). Pour oil in electric wok* and preheat, uncovered, at medium heat about 2 minutes. Add chicken and cook in oil until white (about 5 minutes), stirring constantly. Push chicken up the side. Add broccoli flowerets and strips; cook 5 minutes, stirring constantly. Add additional oil if necessary. Push broccoli up the side. Add mushrooms; cook 1 minute, stirring constantly. Push mushrooms up the side. Stir in remaining ingredients. Heat; stir occasionally. Makes about 6 cups.

*A 10″ skillet may be substituted for a wok.

STOPWATCH BEEF 'n' NOODLE SKILLET

1 pound ground beef
1 medium onion, chopped
1 can (10½ ounces) condensed onion soup
1 to 1½ soup cans water
3 cups uncooked fine noodles
¼ cup chili sauce

In skillet, brown beef and cook onion until tender (use shortening if necessary). Stir to separate meat; pour off fat. Stir in remaining ingredients. Bring to boil; cover. Reduce heat; simmer 5 minutes or until noodles are done. Stir often. Makes about 5 cups.

WHEN IS A* "SPECIAL" *NOT SO SPECIAL? *When the quality is poor. For instance, lean meat at regular price is a better buy than very fatty, bony meat on sale. Low price is not always high value.*

So be flexible. If you see something that's an even better buy than what's on your list, substitute, substitute, substitute.

CHINESE STEW

½ cup diced luncheon meat
1 cup diagonally sliced celery
2 tablespoons butter or margarine
1 can (19 ounces) chunky chicken with rice soup
2 tablespoons sliced green onions
1 tablespoon soy sauce
1 tablespoon cornstarch
2 tablespoons water
Chinese noodles

In saucepan, brown luncheon meat and cook celery in butter until tender. Add soup, onion, and soy. Blend cornstarch and water until smooth; add to soup mixture. Cook, stirring until thickened. Serve over noodles with additional soy. Makes about 3 cups.

COUPONS, COUPONS, COUPONS: Cents off *coupons are great for items that you normally buy or have been wanting to try. But think: do you really need it? If not, it's no bargain, even with a coupon.*

CHICKEN SORRENTO

2 pounds chicken parts
2 tablespoons shortening
1 can (10½ ounces) condensed consommé
½ cup chopped canned tomatoes
1 medium onion, quartered
½ teaspoon oregano leaves, crushed
¼ teaspoon salt
Generous dash pepper
¼ cup water
2 tablespoons flour
Cooked rice or noodles

In skillet, brown chicken in shortening; pour off fat. Add consommé, tomatoes, onion, and seasonings. Cover; cook over low heat 45 minutes or until done. Gradually blend water into flour until smooth; slowly stir into sauce. Cook, stirring until thickened. Serve with rice. Makes 4 servings.

QUICK SKILLET STEW

1 can (about 16 ounces) small whole white potatoes
1 can (11 ounces) condensed Cheddar cheese soup
1 can (12 ounces) luncheon meat, cubed
1 can (about 8 ounces) sliced carrots, drained
2 tablespoons instant minced onion
½ teaspoon prepared mustard
⅛ teaspoon garlic powder

Drain potatoes, reserving ⅓ cup liquid; slice. In skillet, combine potatoes and reserved liquid with remaining ingredients. Heat; gently stir occasionally. Makes about 5 cups.

Fanciful Franks—recipe page 42

PEA PATCH CHICKEN

2 pounds chicken parts
2 tablespoons shortening
1 can (10¾ ounces) condensed golden mushroom soup
1 cup sliced onion
½ teaspoon salt
1 package (10 ounces) frozen peas, cooked and drained

In skillet, brown chicken in shortening; pour off fat. Stir in soup, onion, and salt. Cover; cook over low heat 45 minutes or until done. Stir occasionally. Add peas; heat. Makes 4 servings.

APRICOT PORK CHOPS

1 can (about 8 ounces) unpeeled apricot halves
6 pork chops (about 1½ pounds)
1 can (10¾ ounces) condensed cream of chicken soup
⅓ cup sour cream
2 tablespoons chopped green onions
Cooked rice or noodles

Drain apricots reserving ¼ cup syrup. Cut apricots in half. In skillet, brown chops (use shortening if necessary); pour off fat. Stir in soup, sour cream, reserved syrup, and green onions. Cover; cook over low heat 25 minutes or until done. Stir occasionally. Add apricots; cook 5 minutes more. Serve with rice. Makes 4 servings.

BEEF AND POTATOES AU GRATIN

1 pound ground beef
1 medium onion, chopped
1 can (11 ounces) condensed Cheddar cheese soup
⅓ cup water
1 can (about 16 ounces) small whole white potatoes, drained and sliced

In skillet, brown beef and cook onion until tender (use shortening if necessary). Stir to separate meat; pour off fat. Blend in soup and water; add potatoes. Heat; stir occasionally. Makes about 4 cups.

Stuffed Shells Neapolitan—recipe page 72

MEATBALLS DIABLO

1 can (10¾ ounces) condensed cream of mushroom soup
1 pound ground beef
1 egg, slightly beaten
¼ cup fine dry bread crumbs
¼ cup finely chopped onion
1 tablespoon prepared mustard
1 tablespoon Worcestershire
2 teaspoons prepared horseradish
½ cup water

Mix *thoroughly* ¼ cup soup and remaining ingredients except water. Shape into 16 meatballs. In skillet, brown meatballs (use shortening if necessary); pour off fat. Stir in remaining soup and water. Cover; cook over low heat 20 minutes or until done. Stir occasionally. Makes about 3½ cups.

SAUCY LINKS

1 package (8 ounces) brown 'n serve sausage links
1 can (10¾ ounces) condensed cream of mushroom or celery soup
½ cup milk
½ teaspoon prepared mustard
2 tablespoons chopped parsley
2 cups sliced cooked potatoes
1 cup sliced cooked carrots

In skillet, brown sausage; pour off fat. Stir in soup, milk, mustard, and parsley. Add potatoes and carrots. Heat; stir occasionally. Makes about 4 cups.

LABELS ARE A SHOPPER'S BEST FRIEND! *Read them to find net weight, price, grade, product description, ingredients (listed by weight in descending order) and suggestions for preparation.*

EASY BURGOO

4 link sausage (about ½ pound)
2 pounds chicken parts
1 can (10¾ ounces) condensed cream of chicken soup
½ cup chopped onion
1 small clove garlic, minced
¼ teaspoon rubbed sage
1 can (15½ ounces) kidney beans, drained
2 medium zucchini, cut in ½-inch slices (about 2 cups)

In skillet, slowly brown sausage; remove. Pour off all but 2 tablespoons drippings. Brown chicken in drippings; pour off fat. Add soup, onion, garlic, sage, and sausage. Cover; cook over low heat 30 minutes. Add beans and zucchini. Cook 15 minutes more or until done. Stir occasionally. Makes 4 servings.

LIGHTNING SPAGHETTI

1 pound ground beef
1 medium onion, chopped
1 can (10¾ ounces) condensed tomato soup
1 can (15 ounces) spaghetti in tomato sauce with cheese
Grated Parmesan cheese

In skillet, brown beef and cook onion until tender (use shortening if necessary). Stir to separate meat; pour off fat. Add soup and spaghetti. Heat; stir occasionally. Serve with cheese. Makes about 4½ cups.

GREAT GOULASH

1½ pounds sirloin beef cubes (1 inch)
2 tablespoons shortening
1 can (10¾ ounces) condensed golden mushroom soup
1 teaspoon paprika
½ cup sour cream
Cooked noodles

In skillet, brown beef in shortening; pour off fat. Blend in soup and paprika. Cover; cook over low heat 1 hour or until done. Stir occasionally. Gradually stir in sour cream; heat. Serve over noodles. Makes about 3 cups.

GOLD COAST PORK CHOPS

6 pork chops (about 1½ pounds)
1 can (10¾ ounces) condensed golden mushroom soup
¼ cup water
1 cup carrots thinly sliced diagonally
½ cup chopped onion
Generous dash rubbed sage
1 small green pepper, cut in strips

In skillet, brown chops (use shortening if necessary); pour off fat. Stir in soup, water, carrots, onion, and sage. Cover; cook over low heat 15 minutes. Add green pepper; cook 15 minutes more or until done. Stir occasionally. Makes 4 servings.

TIAJUANA PORK CHOPS

6 pork chops (about 1½ pounds)
1 can (10¾ ounces) condensed cream of celery soup
1 teaspoon chili powder
⅛ teaspoon garlic salt
1 cup canned chick peas
1 cup green pepper squares (1 inch)

In skillet, brown chops (use shortening if necessary); pour off fat. Add soup, chili, and garlic salt. Cover; cook over low heat 15 minutes. Add peas and pepper. Cook 15 minutes more or until done; stir occasionally. Makes 4 servings.

MASON-DIXON SUPPER

1 can (12 ounces) luncheon meat, cubed
⅓ cup diagonally sliced celery
¼ cup chopped onion
2 tablespoons butter or margarine
1 can (10¾ ounces) condensed chicken broth
¾ cup water
¾ cup raw regular rice
1 can (about 8 ounces) sliced peaches, drained

In saucepan, brown luncheon meat and cook celery and onion in butter until tender. Stir in broth, water, and rice. Bring to boil; reduce heat. Cover; cook 20 minutes or until rice is done. Stir occasionally. Add peaches; heat. Makes about 4½ cups.

HOT DEVILED EGGS

4 slices bacon
6 hard-cooked eggs
1 can (10¾ ounces) condensed cream of chicken soup
⅛ teaspoon dry mustard
Generous dash pepper
1 can (about 4 ounces) sliced mushrooms, drained
½ cup water
¼ cup shredded sharp Cheddar cheese
1 tablespoon dried chives
4 English muffins, split and toasted

In skillet, cook bacon until crisp; remove and crumble. Pour off all but 2 tablespoons drippings. Meanwhile, cut eggs in half lengthwise; carefully remove and mash yolks. Mix yolks with 2 tablespoons soup, crumbled bacon, mustard, and pepper. Fill egg whites with yolk mixture. In skillet, lightly brown mushrooms in drippings. Add remaining soup, water, cheese, and chives. Arrange eggs in soup mixture. Cover; cook over low heat until eggs are hot and cheese melts. Stir gently, spooning sauce over eggs. Serve on muffins. Makes 4 servings.

CHINESE SUPPER SKILLET

1 pound ground beef
1 medium onion, chopped
2 cans (10¾ ounces each) condensed golden mushroom soup
½ cup water
1 can (16 ounces) Chinese vegetables, drained
1 cup quick-cooking rice, uncooked
1 teaspoon soy sauce

In skillet, brown beef and cook onion until tender (use shortening if necessary). Stir to separate meat; pour off fat. Add remaining ingredients; bring to boil. Cover. Reduce heat; cook 10 minutes or until rice is done. Stir often. Serve with additional soy. Makes about 6 cups.

MAKING A LIST, CHECKING IT TWICE: *Your budget will think you're Santa Claus if you acquire the habit of shopping with a list.*

First, scan newspapers for advertised specials. Then plan menus for at least a week around bargains that the family enjoys.

Next, check pantry and refrigerator/freezer for needed items. And finally, make a detailed shopping list according to store layout.

SKILLET STEAK AND RICE

1½ pounds boneless round steak (¾-inch thick)
2 tablespoons shortening
1 can (10¾ ounces) condensed golden mushroom soup
1 cup water
½ cup Burgundy or other dry red wine
½ cup sliced onion
¼ teaspoon salt
1½ cups quick-cooking rice, uncooked
1 package (10 ounces) frozen Brussels sprouts, cooked and drained

Pound steak; cut into serving-size pieces. In skillet, brown steak in shortening; pour off fat. Add soup, water, wine, onion, and salt. Cover; cook over low heat 1 hour 15 minutes. Stir occasionally. Add rice and Brussels sprouts; bring to boil. Reduce heat; cover. Cook 10 minutes or until done. Makes 4 servings.

LOUISIANA CHICKEN

2 slices bacon
½ cup chopped onion
1 small green pepper, sliced
⅛ teaspoon thyme leaves, crushed
1 can (10¾ ounces) condensed tomato soup
½ cup water
1½ cups diced cooked chicken
Cooked rice

In skillet, cook bacon until crisp; remove and crumble. Cook onion and pepper with thyme in bacon drippings until tender. Stir in soup, water, and chicken. Heat; stir occasionally. Serve over rice. Garnish with bacon. Makes about 3 cups.

HAMBURGER RISOTTO

1 pound ground beef
½ cup chopped onion
1 can (10¾ ounces) condensed tomato soup
1½ cups water
1½ cups quick-cooking rice, uncooked
1 medium clove garlic, minced
1 teaspoon oregano leaves, crushed
1 teaspoon salt
3 medium zucchini (about ¾ pound), cut in ¼-inch slices
Grated Parmesan cheese

In skillet, brown beef and cook onion until tender (use shortening if necessary); stir to separate meat. Pour off fat. Add remaining ingredients except cheese. Bring to boil; cover. Reduce heat; simmer 10 minutes or until rice is done. Stir often. Serve with Parmesan. Makes about 6 cups.

SAUSAGE SKILLET ROMA

2 medium zucchini (about ½ pound), cut in half lengthwise
1 pound bulk sausage
1 can (10¾ ounces) condensed cream of mushroom soup
½ cup thinly sliced onion
1 medium clove garlic, minced
1 medium tomato, cut in wedges

Cut squash into 1-inch pieces. Shape sausage into 16 meatballs. In skillet, brown sausage; pour off fat. Add remaining ingredients except tomato. Cover; cook over low heat 15 minutes or until done. Stir occasionally. Add tomatoes; cook 5 minutes more. Makes about 4 cups.

FLOUR POWER: *Keep flour in an airtight container since it tends to absorb odors, take up moisture, and dry out easily, depending on conditions.*

To avoid unwanted guests—insects—store in a cool place.

Whole wheat flour? Give it a home in the refrigerator since natural oils cause it to turn rancid quickly at room temperature.

FANCIFUL FRANKS

½ pound frankfurters, cut in 1-inch pieces
½ cup chopped onion
1 teaspoon oregano leaves, crushed
2 tablespoons butter or margarine
1 can (11¼ ounces) condensed chili beef soup
1 can (15 ounces) spaghetti in tomato sauce with cheese

In saucepan, brown frankfurters and cook onion with oregano in butter until tender. Stir in soup and spaghetti. Heat; stir occasionally. Makes about 3½ cups.

JAMBALAYA

8 link sausage (about ½ pound)
1 can (10½ ounces) condensed beef broth
1 cup cubed cooked ham
½ cup raw regular rice
½ cup chopped canned tomatoes
1 small clove garlic, minced
1 package (9 ounces) frozen cut green beans

In skillet, brown sausage. Pour off fat. Add remaining ingredients except beans. Bring to boil; reduce heat. Cover; cook 10 minutes. Add beans; cook 10 minutes more or until done. Stir occasionally. Makes about 4 cups.

CHILI CHOPS

6 pork chops (about 1½ pounds)
Salt
Pepper
1 can (10¾ ounces) condensed tomato soup
1 can (15½ ounces) kidney beans, undrained
½ cup sliced onion
1 tablespoon chili powder
1 large clove garlic, minced
6 green pepper rings
Cooked rice

In skillet, brown chops (use shortening if necessary); pour off fat. Season with salt and pepper. Add remaining ingredients except green pepper and rice. Cover; cook over low heat 15 minutes. Top each chop with green pepper ring. Cook 15 minutes more or until done. Stir occasionally. Serve with rice. Makes 4 servings.

POACHED EGGS LUMBERJACK STYLE

1 pound ground beef
1 medium onion, chopped
2 cans (10¾ ounces each) condensed cream of potato soup
¼ cup water
⅛ teaspoon celery salt
4 eggs

In skillet, brown beef and cook onion until tender (use shortening if necessary); stir to separate meat. Pour off fat. Blend in soup, water, and celery salt; bring to boil. Gently slip eggs into soup mixture. Cover; cook over low heat until whites are firm. Makes 4 servings.

CHICKEN SKILLET GARNI

2 pounds chicken legs
2 tablespoons shortening
1 can (10¾ ounces) condensed cream of chicken soup
⅛ teaspoon ground thyme
½ cup diced carrots
¼ cup chopped celery
¼ cup sliced green onions
¼ cup chopped green pepper

In skillet, brown chicken in shortening; pour off fat. Add soup and thyme. Cover; cook over low heat 15 minutes. Add remaining ingredients. Cook 30 minutes more or until done. Stir occasionally. Makes 4 servings.

SAUSAGE CABBAGE SKILLET

1 pound mild Italian sausage, cut in 1-inch pieces
1 can (10¾ ounces) condensed tomato soup
1 soup can water
2 cups coarsely chopped cabbage
1 package (9 ounces) frozen cut green beans
½ teaspoon basil leaves, crushed
⅛ teaspoon garlic salt
½ cup uncooked elbow macaroni

In skillet, brown sausage; pour off fat. Add remaining ingredients. Bring to boil; reduce heat. Cover; simmer 20 minutes or until done. Stir often. Makes about 5½ cups.

PORK CHOPS JARDINIER

6 pork chops (about 1½ pounds)
1 can (10¾ ounces) condensed cream of mushroom soup
¼ cup water
⅛ teaspoon pepper
⅛ teaspoon thyme leaves, crushed
1 can (about 16 ounces) lima beans, drained
½ cup drained chopped canned tomatoes

In skillet, brown chops; pour off fat. Add soup, water, and seasonings. Cover; cook over low heat 30 minutes or until done. Stir occasionally. Add beans and tomatoes; heat. Makes 4 servings.

CHICKEN CROQUETTES

1 can (10¾ ounces) condensed cream of chicken soup
1½ cups finely chopped cooked chicken
¼ cup fine dry bread crumbs
2 tablespoons finely chopped celery
1 tablespoon finely chopped onion
¼ teaspoon poultry seasoning
Shortening
½ cup milk

To make croquettes, combine ⅓ cup soup, chicken, bread crumbs, celery, onion, and ⅛ teaspoon poultry seasoning. Mix well; shape into 6 croquettes or patties (if mixture is difficult to handle, chill before shaping). Roll in additional bread crumbs. In skillet, brown croquettes in shortening. Meanwhile, in saucepan, combine remaining soup, ⅛ teaspoon poultry seasoning, and milk. Heat; stir occasionally. Serve with croquettes. Makes 3 servings.

FOIL THAT SPOIL: *Wash fresh fruit and mushrooms before eating—not before storing. Moisture encourages spoilage. Store in refrigerator in crisper or moisture-resistant wrap or containers.*

SPAGHETTI with MEAT SAUCE

½ pound ground beef
1 cup chopped onion
1 teaspoon basil leaves, crushed
1 teaspoon oregano leaves, crushed
1 large clove garlic, minced
1 can (10¾ ounces) condensed golden mushroom soup
1 can (10¾ ounces) condensed tomato soup
1 can (16 ounces) tomatoes
¼ cup water
Cooked spaghetti
Grated Parmesan cheese

In saucepan, brown beef and cook onion with seasonings until tender (use shortening if necessary); stir to separate meat. Add soups, tomatoes, and water. Stir to break up tomatoes. Simmer 30 minutes; stir occasionally. Serve over spaghetti with Parmesan. Makes about 4½ cups.

MEXICAN FRICASSEE

½ cup chopped green pepper
½ cup chopped onion
2 tablespoons butter or margarine
1 can (11¼ ounces) condensed chili beef soup
1 can (10¾ ounces) condensed tomato soup
½ cup water
2 cups cubed cooked beef
Cooked rice
Shredded Cheddar cheese

In saucepan, cook green pepper and onion in butter until tender. Stir in soups, water, and beef. Heat; stir occasionally. Serve on rice. Garnish with cheese. Makes about 5 cups.

***TO MARKET, TO MARKET, BUT NOT TOO OFTEN:** Each trip to the store means money spent for gas and another opportunity to buy extras that catch your eye. So shop as infrequently as your freezer and cupboard space allow.*

LEFT BANK CHICKEN

3 pounds chicken parts
3 tablespoons shortening
2 cans (11 ounces each) condensed Cheddar cheese soup
1 can (16 ounces) tomatoes, drained and chopped
1 cup sliced onion
1 teaspoon dried dill weed, crushed
1 teaspoon salt
1 package (9 ounces) frozen cut green beans
1 package (10 ounces) frozen cauliflower
¼ cup water
1 to 2 tablespoons flour
Cooked noodles

In large heavy pan, brown chicken in shortening; pour off fat. Add soup, tomatoes, onion, and seasonings. Cover; cook over low heat 25 minutes. Add beans and cauliflower; cook 20 minutes more or until done. Stir occasionally. Remove chicken and vegetables to serving dish. Gradually blend water into flour until smooth; slowly stir into sauce. Cook, stirring until thickened. Serve with chicken mixture and noodles. Makes 6 servings.

CHICKEN PAPRIKA

2 pounds chicken parts
2 tablespoons shortening
1 can (10¾ ounces) condensed cream of chicken soup
1 tablespoon lemon juice
½ teaspoon paprika

In skillet, brown chicken in shortening; pour off fat. Stir in remaining ingredients. Cover; cook over low heat 45 minutes or until done. Stir occasionally. Makes 4 servings.

TALLYHO MEATBALLS

1 pound ground beef
½ pound liverwurst
1 egg, slightly beaten
1 slice white bread, crumbled
¼ cup finely chopped onion
Generous dash pepper
4 slices bacon
1 can (10¾ ounces) condensed cream of mushroom soup
⅓ cup water
½ cup sour cream

Mix *thoroughly* beef, liverwurst, egg, bread, onion, and pepper; shape into 24 meatballs. In skillet, cook bacon until crisp; remove and crumble. Brown meatballs in drippings; pour off fat. Stir in soup and water. Cover; cook over low heat 15 minutes. Stir in sour cream and bacon; cook 5 minutes more or until done. Stir occasionally. Makes about 4 cups.

FIVE O'CLOCK FRANKS

1 pound frankfurters, cut in thirds
½ cup chopped onion
2 tablespoons butter or margarine
1 can (11 ounces) condensed Cheddar cheese soup
⅓ cup water
2 cups cooked noodles
1 package (9 ounces) frozen cut green beans, cooked and drained
2 tablespoons ketchup

In skillet, brown frankfurters and cook onion in butter until tender. Add remaining ingredients. Heat; stir occasionally. Makes about 6 cups.

CHICKEN HAWAIIAN

2 whole chicken breasts (about 1½ pounds), split
2 tablespoons shortening
1 can (10¾ ounces) condensed cream of chicken soup
¼ cup water
½ cup green pepper strips
½ cup thinly sliced green onions
½ cup drained pineapple chunks
⅛ teaspoon ground ginger

In skillet, brown chicken in shortening; pour off fat. Add remaining ingredients. Cover; cook over low heat 30 minutes or until done. Makes 4 servings.

AN OPEN-SHUT CASE FOR SAVINGS: *Cold air belongs* ***inside*** *your refrigerator and freezer, so open doors only long enough to remove food and drink, then close firmly.*

SUNSHINE CHICKEN

2 pounds chicken parts
2 tablespoons shortening
1 can (10¾ ounces) condensed golden mushroom soup
⅓ cup drained chopped canned tomatoes
½ cup sliced onion
⅛ teaspoon basil leaves, crushed
Cooked rice

In skillet, brown chicken in shortening; pour off fat. Add remaining ingredients except rice. Cover; cook over low heat 45 minutes or until done. Stir occasionally. Serve with rice. Makes 4 servings.

GERMAN STUFFED PORK CHOPS

¼ cup finely chopped onion
1 medium clove garlic, minced
2 tablespoons butter or margarine
1 cup dry rye bread cubes
¼ cup chopped parsley
4 thick pork chops (about 1½ pounds)
1 can (10¾ ounces) condensed golden mushroom soup
½ cup sour cream
¼ cup water
⅛ teaspoon caraway seed
1 medium apple, cut in eighths

To make stuffing, in saucepan, cook onion with garlic in butter until tender; add bread and parsley. Trim excess fat from chops. Slit each chop from outer edge toward bone making a pocket; stuff with bread mixture. Fasten with toothpicks or skewers. In skillet, brown chops (use shortening if necessary); pour off fat. Blend in soup, sour cream, water, and caraway. Cover; cook over low heat 1 hour 15 minutes or until done; stir occasionally. Add apple; heat. Makes 4 servings.

SALISBURY STEAK

1 can (10½ ounces) condensed onion soup
1½ pounds ground beef
½ cup fine dry bread crumbs
1 egg, slightly beaten
¼ teaspoon salt
Dash pepper
¼ cup ketchup
1 teaspoon Worcestershire
½ teaspoon prepared mustard
¼ cup water
1 tablespoon flour

Mix *thoroughly* ⅓ cup soup, beef, bread crumbs, egg, salt, and pepper. Shape into 6 oval patties. In skillet, brown patties (use shortening if necessary); pour off fat. Add remaining soup, ketchup, Worcestershire, and mustard. Gradually blend water into flour until smooth. Stir into soup mixture. Cover; cook over low heat 20 minutes or until done. Stir occasionally. Makes 6 servings.

TANGY POTATO MEATBALLS

1 can (10¾ ounces) condensed tomato soup
1 pound ground beef
½ cup instant mashed potato flakes or puffs
1 egg, slightly beaten
¼ cup finely chopped onion
1 teaspoon salt
1 tablespoon shortening
¼ cup water
1 teaspoon prepared mustard
1 small clove garlic, minced

Mix *thoroughly* ¼ cup soup, beef, potato flakes, egg, onion, and salt. Shape *firmly* into 16 meatballs. Brown meatballs in shortening; pour off fat. Blend in remaining soup, water, mustard, and garlic. Cover; cook over low heat 20 minutes or until done. Stir occasionally. Makes about 4 cups.

GRECIAN LAMB SKILLET

2 cups cubed eggplant (½ medium)
⅓ cup chopped green pepper
1 medium clove garlic, minced
¼ teaspoon thyme leaves, crushed
2 tablespoons butter or margarine
1 can (10¾ ounces) condensed tomato soup
1 soup can water
1½ cups cooked lamb cut in strips
1⅓ cups quick-cooking rice, uncooked

In skillet, cook eggplant and green pepper with garlic and thyme in butter until tender. Add remaining ingredients. Bring to boil; reduce heat. Cover; cook 10 minutes or until rice is done. Stir occasionally. Makes about 5½ cups.

MILK AND MONEY: *Non fat dry milk costs about half as much as fluid whole milk, so your money-saving strategy is easy:*

Keep a supply of reconstituted non fat dry milk in the refrigerator ***for cooking*** *(you can't tell the difference) and* ***for drinking*** *(the secret is keep it COLD). Or mix equal parts of whole milk and reconstituted dry milk if that suits your beverage tastebuds better.*

CHICKEN CRÉCY

2 pounds chicken parts
2 tablespoons shortening
1 can (10¾ ounces) condensed golden mushroom soup
1 cup sliced carrots
½ cup chopped onion
⅛ teaspoon ground nutmeg

In skillet, brown chicken in shortening; pour off fat. Add remaining ingredients. Cover; cook over low heat 45 minutes or until done. Stir occasionally. Makes 4 servings.

PORK CHOPS WITH PIZZAZ

6 pork chops (about 1½ pounds), well-trimmed
Salt
Pepper
1 can (10¾ ounces) condensed chicken broth
¼ teaspoon hot pepper sauce
3 cups uncooked fine noodles, broken in pieces
1 cup chopped canned tomatoes

In skillet, brown chops (use shortening if necessary); pour off fat. Season with salt and pepper. Add broth and hot pepper sauce. Cover; cook over low heat 15 minutes. Add noodles and tomatoes; cook 15 minutes more or until done. Stir often. Makes 4 servings.

ONION STEAK

¼ cup flour
¼ teaspoon salt
Dash pepper
1½ pounds round steak (¾-inch thick)
2 tablespoons shortening
1 can (10½ ounces) condensed onion soup
½ cup ketchup
1 medium green pepper, cut in strips

Combine flour and seasonings; pound into steak. Cut steak into serving-size pieces. In skillet, brown steak in shortening; pour off fat. Add soup and ketchup. Cover; cook over low heat 1 hour 15 minutes. Add green pepper; cook 15 minutes more or until done. Stir occasionally. Makes 4 servings.

CHILI BEEF HASH

1 pound ground beef
3 cups diced raw potatoes
1 cup sliced celery
2 tablespoons shortening
1 can (10¾ ounces) condensed golden mushroom soup
½ cup water
¼ cup chili sauce
½ teaspoon salt
Generous dash pepper

In skillet, brown beef and cook potatoes and celery in shortening; stir to separate meat. Pour off fat. Add remaining ingredients. Cover; cook over low heat 10 minutes. Stir occasionally. Makes about 4½ cups.

CHICKEN SALERNO

- **¼ pound mild Italian sausage, sliced**
- **1 cup zucchini slices cut in half**
- **1 small clove garlic, minced**
- **1 can (19 ounces) chunky chicken soup**
- **½ cup drained chopped canned tomatoes**
- **1 tablespoon cornstarch**
- **2 tablespoons water**
- **Italian bread slices, toasted**
- **Grated Parmesan cheese**

In saucepan, cook sausage until done; add zucchini and garlic. Cook until zucchini is tender. Add soup and tomatoes. Blend cornstarch and water; add to soup mixture. Cook over low heat, stirring until thickened. Serve over Italian bread sprinkled with cheese. Makes about 3 cups.

CHEESE-SMOTHERED CHICKEN

- **2 pounds chicken parts**
- **2 tablespoons butter or margarine**
- **1 can (11 ounces) condensed Cheddar cheese soup**
- **½ cup cut-up canned tomatoes**
- **⅓ cup finely chopped onion**
- **¼ teaspoon basil leaves, crushed**

In skillet, slowly brown chicken in butter (about 30 minutes). Add remaining ingredients. Cover; cook over low heat 15 minutes or until done. Stir occasionally. Makes 4 servings.

TIGHT FIT: *Are the gaskets around your refrigerator and freezer doors worn out or ill-fitting? If so, they can run up operating costs by letting cold air out and warm air in.*

To test for tightness, place a dollar bill between the gasket and the cabinet. Close the door normally. Pull the dollar bill straight out—there should be at least a slight drag.

Test all around the door, including the side hinge. No drag in places? Call a serviceman to check the gasket and door for alignment.

INDIVIDUAL CANTONESE STEAKS

1½ pounds boneless round steak (¾-inch thick)
2 tablespoons shortening
1 can (10½ ounces) condensed beef broth
¾ cup water
1 tablespoon soy sauce
1 large green pepper, cut in strips
3 tablespoons cornstarch
Cooked rice

Cut meat into serving-size pieces. In skillet, brown meat in shortening; pour off fat. Add broth, ½ cup water, and soy. Cover; cook over low heat 1 hour 15 minutes. Add green pepper; cook 10 minutes more or until done. Stir occasionally. Blend ¼ cup water and cornstarch until smooth; slowly stir into sauce. Cook, stirring until thickened. Serve with rice and additional soy. Makes 4 servings.

SPICY HOT CHICKEN SKILLET

2 pounds chicken parts
2 tablespoons shortening
1 can (10¾ ounces) condensed tomato soup
1 cup sliced onion
1 large clove garlic, minced
2 teaspoons chili powder
⅛ teaspoon ground cinnamon
Generous dash crushed red pepper
¼ cup sliced pimiento-stuffed olives
1 large green pepper, cut in strips
Cooked rice

In skillet, brown chicken in shortening; pour off fat. Add remaining ingredients except olives, green pepper, and rice. Cover; cook over low heat 35 minutes. Add olives and green pepper. Cook 10 minutes more or until done. Stir occasionally. Serve with rice. Makes 4 servings.

THE HUNGRY EYE: *Never shop on an empty stomach. Studies show that the hungry shopper sees more that looks appealing and buys accordingly—with budget-battering results.*

CHICKEN ZUCCHINI SKILLET

2 pounds chicken parts
2 tablespoons shortening
1 can (10¾ ounces) condensed cream of mushroom soup
½ cup well-drained chopped canned tomatoes
1 medium clove garlic, minced
⅛ teaspoon Italian seasoning, crushed
2 medium zucchini, sliced (about 1 pound)
Cooked rice
Grated Parmesan cheese

In skillet, brown chicken in shortening; pour off fat. Add soup, tomatoes, garlic, and seasoning. Cover; cook over low heat 30 minutes. Add squash; cook 15 minutes more or until done. Stir occasionally. Uncover; cook to desired consistency. Serve with rice; garnish with cheese. Makes 4 servings.

TEXAS MEATBALLS

1 pound ground beef
½ pound bulk sausage
½ cup soft bread crumbs
1 egg, slightly beaten
1 can (10½ ounces) condensed onion soup
1 can (10¾ ounces) condensed tomato soup
2 tablespoons cornstarch
2 large cloves garlic, minced
¼ cup vinegar
3 tablespoons brown sugar
1 tablespoon Worcestershire
⅛ teaspoon hot pepper sauce
Cooked rice

Mix *thoroughly* beef, sausage, crumbs, and egg. Shape into 24 meatballs. In skillet, brown meatballs; pour off fat. Add remaining ingredients except rice. Cover; cook over low heat 20 minutes or until done. Stir occasionally. Serve with rice. Makes about 5 cups.

AND THE COST CAME TUMBLING DOWN: *You'll be able to spot genuine bargain prices instantly if you keep a week to week list of regular food prices until you become very familiar with them.*

RED FLANNEL PORK HASH

2 cups diced cooked pork
½ cup chopped onion
⅓ cup salad oil
1 package (16 ounces) frozen hash brown potatoes
½ teaspoon salt
Generous dash pepper
1 can (10¾ ounces) condensed cream of chicken soup
1 jar (16 ounces) pickled beets, drained and chopped
¼ cup chopped parsley
Sliced hard-cooked egg

In skillet, brown pork and cook onion in 2 tablespoons oil until tender. Add remaining oil, potatoes, salt, and pepper. Cook 10 minutes. Stir in soup, beets, and parsley. Heat; stir occasionally. Garnish with egg and additional parsley. Makes about 5 cups.

BURGERS 'n' VEGETABLES

1 pound ground beef
¼ cup finely chopped onion
½ teaspoon salt
Generous dash pepper
1 can (10¾ ounces) condensed golden mushroom soup
¼ cup water
1 teaspoon Worcestershire
1 cup thinly sliced carrots
1 package (9 ounces) frozen cut green beans

Mix *thoroughly* beef, onion, salt, and pepper; shape *firmly* into 4 oval patties. In skillet, brown patties (use shortening if necessary); pour off fat. Stir in remaining ingredients. Cover; cook over low heat 20 minutes or until done. Stir occasionally. Makes 4 servings.

PUT YOUR DISHWASHER ON A MAINTENANCE DIET: *Scrape excess food from plates before your dishwasher has a chance to devour it. Debris in the pump can hamper the machine's efficiency. Also, check the filter screen over the drain in the dishwasher regularly and remove any particles.*

FRANKFURTER EXPRESS

- ½ pound frankfurters, cut in ½-inch slices
- 1 small onion, sliced
- 2 tablespoons butter or margarine
- 1 can (10¾ ounces) condensed cream of mushroom soup
- ¼ cup water
- 1 can (16 ounces) small whole white potatoes, drained and diced
- 1 can (8 ounces) cut green beans, drained

In saucepan, brown frankfurters and cook onion in butter until tender. Add soup, water, potatoes, and green beans. Heat; stir occasionally. Makes about 4 cups.

IS THERE A PEEP-SHOW IN YOUR KITCHEN? *If you can't resist looking in the oven every time something is cooking, there is. And the price of admission is a higher utility bill; all that escaping heat mounts up.*

CHEESY TUNA MEDLEY

- 2 slices bacon
- ¼ cup sliced green onions
- ⅛ teaspoon thyme leaves, crushed
- 1 can (11 ounces) condensed Cheddar cheese soup
- 2 tablespoons water
- ½ cup drained cut-up canned tomatoes
- Generous dash pepper
- 2 cups sliced cooked potatoes
- 2 cans (about 7 ounces each) tuna, drained and flaked

In saucepan, cook bacon until crisp; remove and crumble. Pour off all but 2 tablespoons drippings. Cook onion with thyme in drippings until tender. Stir in soup, water, tomatoes, and pepper; add potatoes and tuna. Heat; stir occasionally. Garnish with bacon. Makes about 4½ cups.

MEATBALLS NAPOLI

1 pound meatloaf mix
¼ cup fine dry bread crumbs
¼ cup finely chopped onion
1 egg, slightly beaten
¼ teaspoon salt
Generous dash pepper
1 can (10¾ ounces) condensed cream of chicken soup
1 can (16 ounces) tomatoes, chopped and drained
¼ teaspoon Italian seasoning, crushed
Cooked rice

In bowl, mix *thoroughly* meat, bread crumbs, onion, egg, salt, and pepper. Shape into 16 meatballs. In skillet, brown meatballs (use shortening if necessary); pour off fat. Stir in soup, tomatoes, and seasoning. Cover; cook over low heat 20 minutes or until done. Stir occasionally. Serve with rice. Makes about 4 cups.

SAUSAGE CHUCKWAGON STYLE

1 can (11¼ ounces) condensed chili beef soup
1 can (about 16 ounces) whole green beans
⅔ cup raw regular rice
¼ teaspoon onion salt
2 cans (5 ounces each) Vienna sausage, drained

In saucepan, empty soup. Drain green beans, reserving liquid. Measure green bean liquid in soup can; add enough water to measure 2 soup cans. Gradually stir into soup; add rice and onion salt. Bring to boil; reduce heat. Cover; cook 20 minutes or until rice is done. Stir occasionally. Add sausage and beans; heat. Makes about 6 cups.

A PORK CHOP BY ANY NAME OTHER THAN* "CENTER-CUT" *COSTS LESS: *Rib, blade, arm, and loin end pork chops are every bit as delicious and nutritious as center-cut—and you'll like the change.*

meatless wonders

Step right up folks and taste some amazing main dishes featuring eggs, cheese, and fish. They contain the same high quality protein as meat, but usually cost less. What's more, they are exceptionally delicious and satisfying, as the following recipes demonstrate.

RICE SOUFFLÉ

6 eggs, separated
¼ cup chopped onion
2 teaspoons curry powder
2 tablespoons butter or margarine
1 can (10¾ ounces) condensed cream of mushroom soup
1 cup shredded sharp process cheese
1½ cups cooked rice

Beat egg yolks until thick and lemon-colored. In saucepan, cook onion with curry in butter until tender. Blend in soup and cheese; heat slowly until cheese melts. Stir occasionally. Remove from heat; stir yolks into hot soup mixture. Stir in rice. In large bowl, using clean egg beater, beat egg whites until stiff; fold in soup mixture. Pour into an ungreased 2-quart casserole. Bake at 300°F. for 1 hour to 1 hour 15 minutes or until soufflé is golden brown. Serve immediately. Makes 4 to 6 servings.

SPANISH EGGS

½ cup chopped onion
¼ cup chopped green pepper
1 medium clove garlic, minced
1 tablespoon chili powder
2 tablespoons butter or margarine
1 can (10¾ ounces) condensed tomato soup
⅓ cup water
¼ cup sliced ripe olives
8 eggs
Salt
Pepper
Shredded Cheddar cheese

In saucepan, cook onion and green pepper with garlic and chili in butter until tender. Stir in soup, water, and olives. Cook over low heat 15 minutes; stir occasionally. Pour half of soup mixture into a 2-quart shallow baking dish (12x8x2"); break eggs into sauce. Spoon remaining soup mixture over eggs. Salt and pepper to taste. Bake eggs at 350°F. for 10 to 15 minutes or until set. Garnish with cheese; serve with tortillas. Makes 4 servings.

PUFFY OMELET with CHEESE SAUCE

Omelet:

6 eggs, separated
1/3 cup milk
Dash pepper
3 tablespoons butter or margarine

Sauce:

1 can (10¾ ounces) condensed cream of mushroom soup
½ cup milk
1 cup shredded Swiss cheese
1 package (10 ounces) frozen asparagus spears, cooked and drained

To make omelet: Beat egg yolks until thick and lemon-colored; mix in milk and pepper. Using clean egg beater, beat egg whites until stiff but not dry; fold in yolk mixture. Heat butter in oven-proof skillet; pour in eggs. Cook over low heat about 5 minutes or until lightly browned on bottom. Bake at 350°F. for 10 minutes or until top springs back when pressed with finger.
To make sauce: In saucepan, blend soup and milk; add cheese. Heat until cheese melts. Stir occasionally.
Transfer omelet to heated platter. Make a shallow cut down center; top with asparagus. Fold in half. Serve with sauce; sprinkle with paprika. Makes 4 servings.

GARDEN SKILLET

2 cups diced zucchini
½ cup chopped onion
½ teaspoon basil leaves, crushed
2 tablespoons butter or margarine
1 can (11 ounces) condensed Cheddar cheese soup
3 cups cooked elbow macaroni
2 cups shredded sharp Cheddar cheese
1 can (16 ounces) tomatoes, chopped and well-drained
½ teaspoon prepared mustard

In skillet, cook zucchini and onion with basil in butter until tender. Add remaining ingredients. Heat until cheese melts; stir occasionally. Makes about 5½ cups.

BIG BEAN BONANZA

1 can (16 ounces) tomatoes, chopped
1 cup sliced onion
1 medium clove garlic, minced
1 tablespoon chili powder
2 tablespoons butter or margarine
1 can (11½ ounces) condensed green pea soup
1 can (about 16 ounces) lima beans, drained
1 can (15½ ounces) kidney beans, undrained
1 can (8½ ounces) butter beans, drained
4 slices (about 4 ounces) mild process cheese, cut in half diagonally

In skillet, simmer tomatoes and onion with garlic and chili in butter about 15 minutes or until tender. Stir in soup. Add remaining ingredients except cheese. Heat; stir occasionally. Top with cheese. Cover; heat until cheese melts. Makes about 5½ cups.

STUFFED FLOUNDER ROLL-UPS

2 packages (10 ounces each) frozen broccoli spears, cooked and drained or 4 medium cooked carrots, cut in thin sticks
8 fillets of flounder (2 pounds)
1 can (10¾ ounces) condensed cream of celery soup
¼ cup mayonnaise
1 tablespoon lemon juice

Divide broccoli among fillets; roll up. Secure with toothpicks. Arrange in 2-quart shallow baking dish (12x8x2"). Bake at 350°F. for 20 minutes. Meanwhile, combine remaining ingredients; pour over fish, stirring into liquid around fish. Bake 15 minutes more or until done. Stir sauce before serving. Makes 6 to 8 servings.

PATIO TUNA SALAD

- 1 can (10¾ ounces) condensed cream of shrimp soup
- 2 cups cooked elbow macaroni
- 1 can (about 7 ounces) tuna, drained and flaked
- ½ cup diced green pepper
- 2 tablespoons sliced stuffed olives
- 1 tablespoon finely chopped onion
- 1 tablespoon lemon juice
- Dash pepper

In bowl, combine ingredients; chill. Serve on crisp salad greens. Makes about 4 cups.

TUNA CLAM TEMPTER

- 1 can (19 ounces) chunky clam chowder soup
- 1 can (about 7 ounces) tuna, drained and flaked
- ½ cup cooked whole kernel corn
- ⅛ teaspoon hot pepper sauce
- 1 tablespoon cornstarch
- 2 tablespoons water

In saucepan, combine soup, tuna, corn, and hot pepper sauce. Blend cornstarch and water until smooth; add to soup mixture. Heat, stirring until thickened. Makes about 3½ cups.

TUNA NOODLE PATTIES

- 1 can (10¾ ounces) condensed cream of celery soup
- 2 cans (about 7 ounces each) tuna, drained and flaked
- 1 cup crushed uncooked fine noodles
- ½ cup finely chopped celery
- 2 tablespoons chopped pimiento
- ¼ cup fine dry bread crumbs
- 2 tablespoons butter or margarine
- ¼ cup milk
- 2 tablespoons chopped parsley
- 1 tablespoon lemon juice

In bowl, combine ¼ cup soup, tuna, noodles, celery, and pimiento. Shape into 6 patties; coat with bread crumbs. In skillet, brown patties in butter (add more butter if necessary). Meanwhile, in saucepan, combine remaining soup, milk, parsley, and lemon. Heat; stir occasionally. Serve with patties. Makes 6 servings.

SWISS FONDUE

- 1 can (11 ounces) condensed Cheddar cheese soup
- 1 package (8 ounces) rectangular slices natural Swiss cheese, cut or torn in pieces
- ¼ teaspoon prepared mustard
- ¼ teaspoon Worcestershire
- ¼ teaspoon hot pepper sauce
- French or Italian bread cubes

In saucepan, combine soup, cheese, mustard, Worcestershire, and pepper sauce. Heat until cheese melts. Stir occasionally. Spear bread with fork or toothpick and dip into hot cheese. Makes about 2 cups.

SAVE-ORY SCRAMBLE: *When the price difference between any two sizes of eggs is less than 7 cents, the larger eggs are a better buy than the smaller.*

PLAIN AND FANCY: *What shape is your pasta shelf in? If the good old standbys—elbow macaroni, spaghetti, and noodles–are the extent of your stock, start thinking fancy.*

Unusually shaped pasta may cost slightly more, but it is still one of the least expensive ways to make an otherwise ho-hum meal exciting.

BEFORE-AND-AFTER-THOUGHTS: *Turn oven on AFTER changing rack positions. Turn oven, broiler, and burners off BEFORE removing food. Less energy escapes this way. Less money too.*

LASAGNA MARINARA

⅓ cup very finely chopped onion
¼ teaspoon basil leaves, crushed
⅛ teaspoon thyme leaves, crushed
1 small clove garlic, minced
2 tablespoons salad or olive oil
1 can (10¾ ounces) condensed tomato soup
1 can (about 6 ounces) tomato paste
1½ soup cans water
2 tablespoons grated Parmesan cheese
1 teaspoon salt
1 small bay leaf
9 lasagna noodles (about ½ pound), cooked and drained
2 cups ricotta cheese
1½ cups shredded Mozzarella cheese

In saucepan, cook onion with basil, thyme, and garlic in oil until tender. Blend in soup, tomato paste, water, Parmesan cheese, salt, and bay leaf. Bring to boil; reduce heat. Simmer 30 minutes; stir occasionally. Remove bay leaf. In 2-quart shallow baking dish (12x8x2″), starting with sauce, arrange 3 alternate layers of noodles, ricotta cheese, sauce, and Mozzarella cheese. Sprinkle with additional Parmesan cheese. Bake at 350°F. for 45 minutes or until hot. Let stand 15 minutes before serving. Makes 4 to 6 servings.

POPEYE EGGS 'n' NOODLE BAKE

- 1 can ($10\frac{3}{4}$ ounces) condensed cream of mushroom soup
- ¾ cup water
- 3 tablespoons soy sauce
- ⅛ teaspoon ground ginger
- 6 hard-cooked eggs
- 2 cups cooked noodles
- 1 package (10 ounces) frozen chopped spinach, cooked and drained
- 2 slices tomato, cut in half

In 1½-quart casserole, combine soup, water, soy, and ginger. Chop 5 eggs; slice 1 egg and reserve for garnish. Add chopped eggs, noodles, and spinach to soup mixture. Bake at 400°F. for 25 minutes or until hot; stir. Garnish with tomato and reserved sliced egg. Serve with additional soy sauce. Makes about 5 cups.

SAUCY SWEDISH FISH

- 1 cup carrots sliced diagonally
- ½ cup sliced onion
- ½ teaspoon dill weed, crushed
- 2 tablespoons butter or margarine
- 1 can ($10\frac{3}{4}$ ounces) condensed cream of celery soup
- 1 pound fillets of white fish, cut in 2-inch pieces

In skillet, cook carrots and onion with dill in butter until *just* tender. Add soup and fish. Cover; cook over low heat 10 minutes or until done. Stir occasionally. Makes 4 servings.

NEW ENGLAND SCRAMBLE

½ cup chopped green pepper
¼ cup chopped onion
2 tablespoons butter or margarine
1 can (10¾ ounces) condensed New England clam chowder
8 eggs, slightly beaten
Dash pepper

In 10″ skillet, cook green pepper and onion in butter until tender. In bowl, stir soup until smooth; gradually blend in eggs and pepper. Pour into skillet. Cook over low heat; do not stir. As mixture begins to set around edges, gently lift cooked portions with large turner so that thin, uncooked portion can flow to the bottom. Continue gently lifting cooked portions until eggs are completely set, but still moist (about 8 minutes). Makes 4 servings.

TUNA WAIKIKI

1 can (10¾ ounces) condensed cream of mushroom soup
½ cup milk
2 cans (about 7 ounces each) tuna, drained and flaked
1 cup drained canned pineapple chunks
¼ cup chopped toasted almonds
2 tablespoons finely chopped onion
1 teaspoon soy sauce
4 slices French or Italian bread
2 tablespoons melted butter or margarine
¼ teaspoon dried parsley flakes, crushed

In 1½-quart shallow baking dish (10x6x2″), combine soup, milk, tuna, pineapple, almonds, onion, and soy; top with bread. Brush bread with butter; sprinkle with parsley. Bake at 400°F. for 30 minutes or until hot. Makes about 5 cups.

Yankee Chili—recipe page 95

CHEESY SPINACH 'n' RICE BAKE

½ cup chopped onion
2 tablespoons butter or margarine
1 can (10¾ ounces) condensed cream of mushroom soup
2 cups cooked rice
2 cups shredded sharp Cheddar cheese
1 package (10 ounces) frozen chopped spinach, cooked and well-drained
4 eggs, slightly beaten
¼ teaspoon Worcestershire
⅛ teaspoon thyme leaves, crushed

In saucepan, cook onion in butter until tender. Stir in remaining ingredients. Spoon mixture into 1½-quart shallow baking dish (10x6x2"). Bake at 375°F. for 45 minutes or until set. Makes about 6 cups.

TIME OFF: *Give your refrigerator and freezer a break. If you have a choice, locate them away from heating equipment and direct sunlight so they don't have to work so hard.*

Garden Skillet—recipe page 60

TUNA TOMATO-WICH

1 small green pepper, cut in strips
1 tablespoon butter or margarine
1 can (10¾ ounces) condensed golden mushroom soup
⅓ cup water
1 can (about 7 ounces) tuna, drained and flaked
1 medium tomato, cut in wedges
Toast
Sliced onion

In skillet, cook green pepper in butter until tender. Add soup, water, and tuna. Heat; stir occasionally. Add tomato wedges; heat. Serve on toast. Garnish with onion. Makes about 3 cups.

ALL-IN-ONE TUNA CASSEROLE

1 can (10¾ ounces) condensed cream of onion soup
½ cup sour cream
½ cup milk
2 cups cooked elbow macaroni
1 package (9 ounces) frozen cut green beans, cooked and drained
1 can (about 7 ounces) tuna, drained and flaked
¼ cup diced pimiento
1 tablespoon lemon juice
⅛ teaspoon thyme leaves, crushed
Sliced hard-cooked eggs
Parsley

In 1½-quart casserole, stir soup and sour cream; gradually add milk and remaining ingredients except eggs and parsley. Bake at 400°F. for 30 minutes or until hot; stir. Garnish with eggs and parsley. Makes about 5 cups.

SING A SONG OF SALMON: *But stay in tune with your budget. Color is the clue—the redder the salmon the higher the price. From reddest to pinkest are Sockeye, King, Silver, Pink, and Chum.*

Look at the label and buy right: Pink is ideal for loaves and patties since it breaks into flakes. The deeper reds are good for salads and casseroles since these varieties break into large chunks.

POMPEII TUNA

½ cup diagonally sliced celery
1 medium clove garlic, minced
½ teaspoon oregano leaves, crushed
2 tablespoons butter or margarine
1 can (11 ounces) condensed Cheddar cheese soup
½ cup water
1 can (about 7 ounces) tuna, drained and flaked
2 cups cooked spaghetti
1 cup cooked cut green beans
½ cup chopped canned tomatoes

In saucepan, cook celery with garlic and oregano in butter until tender. Add remaining ingredients. Heat; stir occasionally. Makes about 5 cups.

TUNA TETRAZZINI

2 tablespoons chopped onion
1 tablespoon butter or margarine
1 can (10¾ ounces) condensed cream of mushroom soup
½ cup water
½ cup shredded sharp Cheddar cheese
1 can (about 7 ounces) tuna, drained and flaked
2 tablespoons diced pimiento
1 tablespoon chopped parsley
2 cups cooked spaghetti

In saucepan, cook onion in butter until tender. Blend in soup, water, and cheese. Cook over low heat until cheese melts; stir occasionally. Add tuna, pimiento, parsley, and spaghetti. Heat; stir occasionally. Makes about 3½ cups.

STUFFED SHELLS NEAPOLITAN

1 can (10¾ ounces) condensed cream of celery soup
½ teaspoon lemon juice
¼ teaspoon oregano leaves, crushed
1 package (10 ounces) frozen chopped broccoli, cooked and well-drained
½ cup drained chopped canned tomatoes
1 can (about 7 ounces) tuna, drained and flaked
12 jumbo shells macaroni, cooked and drained
½ cup grated mild Cheddar cheese

Combine soup, lemon juice, oregano, broccoli, tomatoes, and tuna. Stuff about ¼ cup mixture into each shell. In 1½-quart shallow baking dish (10x6x2"); arrange stuffed shells. Bake at 400°F. for 20 minutes or until hot. Sprinkle with cheese; bake 5 minutes more or until cheese melts. Garnish with parsley if desired. Makes 4 servings.

CLAM SPAGHETTI SUPPER

¼ cup chopped onion
1 small clove garlic, minced
1 tablespoon butter or margarine
1 can (19 ounces) chunky clam chowder soup
½ cup uncooked thin spaghetti broken in pieces
½ cup chopped parsley

In saucepan, cook onion with garlic in butter until tender. Add remaining ingredients. Cover; cook over low heat 20 minutes or until spaghetti is done. Stir often. Makes about 2 cups.

RIPE, RIPER, RIPEST: *Ripen tomatoes, avocados, melons, peaches, pears, and plums at room temperature out of direct sunlight. Then refrigerate until ready to use.*

TAKE A CAN OF TUNA: *But which one? So many kinds crowd the market shelves.*

A word to the pennywise: Tuna is priced by ***type****—white is costlier than light. And by* ***pack****—according to the size of the pieces. Fancy-or solid-pack tuna is most expensive, so save it for something special. Chunk tuna comes next—a natural for casseroles since the pieces hold their shape. Flaked tuna makes an ideal sandwich filling because the fish is already in small pieces.*

Choose the tuna that best fits your needs, and remember—all tuna is created nutritionally equal, no matter what the price.

TUNA LOAF WITH HORSERADISH SAUCE

1 can (10¾ ounces) condensed tomato soup
2 cans (about 7 ounces each) tuna, drained and flaked
1 cup small bread cubes
2 eggs, slightly beaten
2 tablespoons chopped parsley
2 teaspoons lemon juice
2 tablespoons water
1 tablespoon prepared horseradish
⅛ teaspoon basil leaves, crushed

Mix *thoroughly* ½ cup soup, tuna, bread cubes, eggs, parsley, and lemon juice. Spread evenly in well-greased loaf pan (8x4x3"). Bake at 400°F. for 40 minutes. Loosen edges; unmold. Meanwhile, combine remaining soup, water, horseradish, and basil. Heat; stir occasionally. Serve with loaf. Makes 6 servings.

TOMATO-MUSHROOM RABBIT

1 can (about 2 ounces) sliced mushrooms, drained
2 tablespoons chopped onion
2 tablespoons butter or margarine
1 can (11 ounces) condensed Cheddar cheese soup
¼ teaspoon prepared mustard
¼ cup milk
Toast
Tomato slices

In saucepan, brown mushrooms and cook onion in butter until tender. Blend in soup and mustard; gradually add milk. Heat; stir occasionally. Top toast with tomato slices; pour sauce over all. Makes about 1½ cups.

YOUR TURN TO WASH? *Soiled dishes needn't take your hot water bill out of sight. Simply avoid running the hot water for long periods.*

Use a pan of sudsy hot water to wash, a pan of plain hot water to rinse . . . glassware first, eating utensils next, followed by plates, and finally, pots and pans.

TUNA A LA KING

½ cup sliced celery
2 tablespoons chopped onion
1 tablespoon butter or margarine
1 can (10¾ ounces) condensed cream of mushroom soup
⅓ cup milk
1 can (about 7 ounces) tuna, drained and flaked
2 tablespoons chopped pimiento
Toast or biscuits

In saucepan, cook celery and onion in butter until tender. Stir in soup, milk, tuna, and pimiento. Heat; stir occasionally. Serve over toast. Garnish with chopped parsley if desired. Makes about 2½ cups.

TUNA NOODLE COMBO

1 can (10¾ ounces) condensed cream of celery soup
½ cup sour cream
½ cup milk
1 can (about 7 ounces) tuna, drained and flaked
2 tablespoons chopped parsley
2 tablespoons chopped pimiento
¼ teaspoon salt
Generous dash pepper
2 cups cooked noodles
2 tablespoons buttered bread crumbs

Blend soup and sour cream; stir in milk. Add tuna, parsley, pimiento, seasonings, and noodles. Pour into 1½-quart casserole. Bake at 400°F. for 25 minutes or until hot; stir. Top with bread crumbs. Bake 5 minutes more. Makes about 4 cups.

TUNA SALAD LAMAZE

1 can (10¾ ounces) condensed tomato soup
1 cup mayonnaise
¼ cup sweet pickle relish
1 tablespoon lemon juice
½ teaspoon grated onion
½ teaspoon prepared mustard
2 cups cubed cooked potatoes
1 package (9 ounces) frozen cut green beans, cooked and drained
1 can (about 7 ounces) tuna, drained and flaked

Combine soup, mayonnaise, relish, lemon, onion, and mustard. Mix 1 cup soup mixture with potatoes and beans. Chill 1 hour or more. Arrange potato mixture on crisp salad greens; top with tuna. Serve with remaining dressing. Makes 4 servings.

EASY OVEN FILLETS

1 pound fillets of white fish (haddock, flounder, or other white fish)
1 can (about 16 ounces) small whole white potatoes, drained
1 can (10¾ ounces) condensed cream of celery soup
2 tablespoons chopped parsley
Paprika

Arrange fish and potatoes in single layer in 2-quart shallow baking dish (12x8x2"). Bake at 350°F. for 15 minutes. Pour soup over, stirring into liquid around fish. Bake 10 minutes more or until done. Stir sauce before serving. Sprinkle with parsley and paprika if desired. Makes 3 servings.

CUPBOARD, CUPBOARD ON THE WALL: *Who's the thriftiest of all? You are, if you can afford the storage space for staples such as canned goods when they're on* special. *If not, consider a do-it-yourself shelf project in some cool, dry spot.*

pot luck

Ahh, the joys of a one-pot supper—simplicity in preparation and cleanup, old-fashioned flavors, tantalizing smells. Dish out some down-home goodness tonight with one of the following stews, roasts, or meal-in-a-bowl soups.

BEEF 'n' BEANS

2 frankfurters, sliced
1 tablespoon butter or margarine
1 can (19 ounces) chunky beef soup
1 can (16 ounces) pork & beans with tomato sauce
2 teaspoons prepared mustard
½ teaspoon prepared horseradish

In saucepan, brown frankfurters in butter. Add remaining ingredients. Heat; stir occasionally. Makes about 4 cups.

SPANISH CHICKEN

2 pounds chicken parts
2 tablespoons shortening
1 can (10¾ ounces) condensed chicken broth
½ cup water
2 medium cloves garlic, minced
1 teaspoon salt
½ cup chopped onion
⅔ cup raw regular rice
1 package (10 ounces) frozen peas
1 cup cut-up canned tomatoes

In skillet, slowly brown chicken in shortening (about 30 minutes); pour off fat. Remove chicken. Stir in remaining ingredients except peas and tomatoes; top with chicken. Cover; cook over low heat 15 minutes. Stir occasionally. Add peas and tomatoes. Cook 10 minutes more or until done. Makes 4 servings.

HAM AND PEA TETRAZZINI

1½ cups cooked ham cut in strips
1 small clove garlic, minced
2 tablespoons butter or margarine
1 can (10¾ ounces) condensed cream of chicken soup
¾ cup milk
1 cup shredded Swiss cheese
1 package (10 ounces) frozen peas, cooked and drained
2 cups cooked spaghetti

In saucepan, brown ham with garlic in butter. Add soup, milk, and cheese. Heat until cheese melts; stir occasionally. Add peas and spaghetti; heat. Makes about 5½ cups.

BRUNSWICK STEW

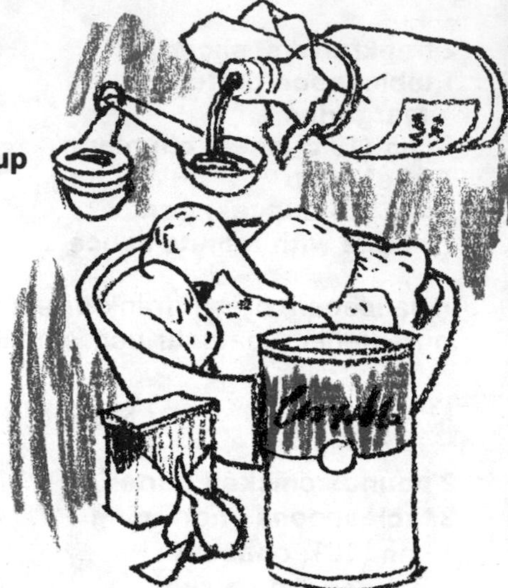

2 slices bacon
2 pounds chicken parts
1 can (10¾ ounces) condensed tomato soup
⅓ cup water
½ cup sliced onion
1 teaspoon Worcestershire
1 medium clove garlic, minced
½ teaspoon salt
Dash pepper
1 package (10 ounces) frozen whole okra
1 package (10 ounces) frozen succotash

In large heavy pan, cook bacon until crisp; remove and crumble. Pour off all but 2 tablespoons drippings. Brown chicken in drippings. Stir in soup, water, onion, Worcestershire, garlic, salt, and pepper. Cover; cook over low heat 15 minutes. Add vegetables. Cook 30 minutes more or until done. Stir occasionally. Spoon off fat. Garnish with bacon. Makes 4 servings.

PROVINCIAL HAM POTAGE

1½ cups diced cooked ham
½ cup chopped onion
¼ teaspoon dried dill weed, crushed
2 tablespoons butter or margarine
1 can (10¾ ounces) condensed cream of celery soup
1 can (10¾ ounces) condensed cream of chicken soup
1 soup can milk
1 soup can water
1 package (9 ounces) French style green beans, cooked and drained
1 cup sliced cooked carrots

In saucepan, brown ham and cook onion with dill in butter until tender. Stir in soups; gradually blend in milk and water. Add remaining ingredients. Heat; stir occasionally. Makes about 7½ cups.

CALICO STEW

- **½ pound bulk sausage**
- **2 pounds chicken parts**
- **1 can (10¾ ounces) condensed tomato soup**
- **¼ cup water**
- **1 teaspoon oregano leaves, crushed**
- **¼ teaspoon paprika**
- **4 ears frozen corn on the cob, thawed and cut in half**

In large heavy pan, brown sausage; stir to separate meat. Remove; drain. Brown chicken in drippings; pour off fat. Add sausage and remaining ingredients except corn. Cover; cook over low heat 25 minutes. Stir occasionally. Add corn; cook 20 minutes more or until done. Makes 4 servings.

NEW MATH: *Cook double and subtract from your utility bill. When you make twice as much spaghetti sauce, Stroganoff, stew, even two casseroles—and freeze part for another meal—you use less heat, and save, save, save. Less work for the chef, too.*

COUNTY FAIR CHICKEN

- **3 pounds chicken parts**
- **2 tablespoons shortening**
- **2 cans (10¾ ounces each) condensed cream of mushroom soup**
- **1½ soup cans water**
- **¼ teaspoon thyme leaves, crushed**
- **¼ teaspoon salt**
- **Generous dash pepper**
- **3 cups uncooked medium noodles**
- **1 package (10 ounces) frozen cut green beans**

In large heavy pan, brown chicken in shortening; pour off fat. Add soup, water, and seasonings. Cover; cook over low heat 30 minutes. Add noodles and green beans. Cook 20 minutes more or until done. Stir occasionally. Makes 6 servings.

BUTTERMILK CHUCK STEW

3½-pound boneless chuck roast (about 2-inch thick)
2 tablespoons shortening
2 cans (10¾ ounces each) condensed cream of mushroom soup
1½ cups buttermilk
¾ cup water
1 cup chopped onion
¼ teaspoon ground nutmeg
⅛ teaspoon pepper
4 medium carrots (about ½ pound), cut in 1½-inch pieces
1 small head cauliflower (about 1 pound), separated into flowerets

Trim fat from meat; cut in 1½-inch cubes. In large heavy oven-proof pan, brown meat in shortening; pour off fat. Stir in soup, buttermilk, water, onion, nutmeg, and pepper. Cover; bake at 350°F. for 1 hour 30 minutes. Add carrots; stir mixture. Bake 30 minutes more. Arrange cauliflower on top of stew; bake 30 minutes more or until done. Garnish with parsley if desired. Makes about 10 cups.

IRISH CHUCK ROAST

3½-pound boneless chuck roast (about 2-inch thick)
2 tablespoons shortening
2 cans (10¾ ounces each) condensed golden mushroom soup
½ cup chopped canned tomatoes
1 tablespoon prepared horseradish
½ teaspoon celery seed
6 small potatoes (about 1½ pounds), cut in half
1 medium head cabbage, cut in 6 wedges

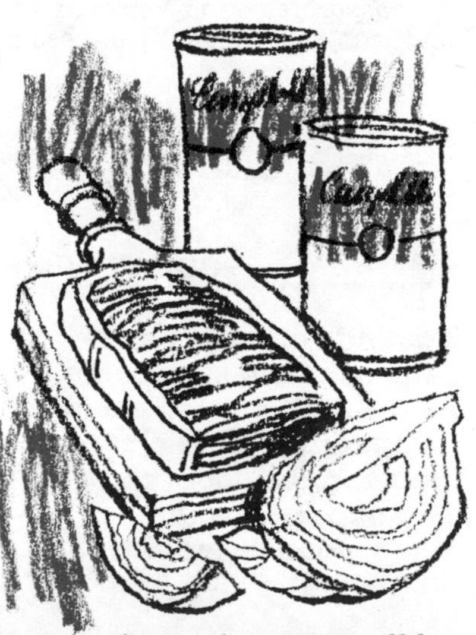

In large heavy pan, brown meat in shortening; pour off fat. Add soup, tomatoes, horseradish, and celery seed. Cover; cook over low heat 2 hours. Add potatoes; place cabbage on top. Cook 1 hour more or until done. Stir occasionally. Spoon off fat; thicken sauce if desired. Makes 6 servings.

PIQUANT BEEF POT

2 cans (10¾ ounces each) condensed cream of potato soup
1 soup can milk
½ soup can water
2 cups cubed cooked beef
½ cup shredded Cheddar cheese
1 package (10 ounces) frozen mixed vegetables, cooked and drained
2 tablespoons chopped parsley
2 teaspoons prepared horseradish

In saucepan, combine ingredients. Heat; stir occasionally. Makes about 7 cups.

LANCASTER COUNTY MEATBALLS

1 pound ground beef
1 egg, slightly beaten
¼ cup fine dry bread crumbs
2 tablespoons finely chopped onion
⅛ teaspoon salt
⅛ teaspoon pepper
2 tablespoons shortening
1 cup thinly sliced carrots
2 cans (10½ ounces each) condensed beef broth
2 soup cans water
1 small bay leaf
1½ cups medium noodles, broken in pieces

Mix *thoroughly* beef, egg, bread crumbs, onion, salt, and pepper; shape into 24 meatballs. In large heavy pan, brown meatballs in shortening; pour off fat. Add remaining ingredients. Bring to boil; reduce heat. Simmer 10 minutes or until noodles are done. Stir occasionally. Remove bay leaf. Garnish with sour cream if desired. Makes about 7 cups.

MINUTEMAN SKILLET

½ cup sliced celery
2 tablespoons butter or margarine
1 can (10¾ ounces) condensed cream of mushroom soup
2 cups cooked rice
1½ cups cubed cooked chicken
1 can (about 8 ounces) sliced carrots, undrained
Grated Parmesan cheese

In skillet, cook celery in butter until tender. Add soup, rice, chicken, and carrots. Heat; stir occasionally. Serve with cheese. Makes about 4 cups.

QUICK CHICKEN CORN CHOWDER

½ cup chopped onion
¼ teaspoon poultry seasoning
⅛ teaspoon pepper
2 tablespoons butter or margarine
1 can (10¾ ounces) condensed cream of chicken soup
1 can (10¾ ounces) condensed cream of potato soup
1 soup can milk
1 soup can water
1½ cups diced cooked chicken
1 can (about 8 ounces) cream style corn

In large saucepan, cook onion with seasonings in butter until tender. Add soups; gradually stir in milk and water. Add chicken and corn. Heat; stir occasionally. Garnish with chopped parsley if desired. Makes about 7 cups.

HEARTY TRIPLE TREAT

1 can (19 ounces) chunky chicken with rice soup
1 can (19 ounces) chunky vegetable soup
1 can (16 ounces) home style beans

In saucepan, combine ingredients. Heat; stir occasionally. Makes about 6 cups.

SPICEBOX STEW

1½ pounds beef cubes (1½ inch)
2 tablespoons shortening
2 cans (10¾ ounces each) condensed tomato soup
½ cup water
½ cup Burgundy or other dry red wine
1 small bay leaf
¼ teaspoon thyme leaves, crushed
3 medium potatoes (about 1 pound), quartered
8 small whole white onions (½ pound)
1 package (10 ounces) frozen peas

In large heavy pan, brown beef in shortening; pour off fat. Add soup, water, Burgundy, bay leaf, and thyme. Cover; cook over low heat 1 hour 30 minutes. Add potatoes and onions. Cook 45 minutes; add peas. Cook 15 minutes more or until done. Stir occasionally. Remove bay leaf. Makes about 8 cups.

THE CHEESE STANDS ALONE: *And for good reason. Store strong-flavored cheeses in tightly covered jars in the refrigerator to prevent their odor from spreading to other foods.*

MEATBALL STEW

1 pound ground beef
1 egg, slightly beaten
½ cup small bread cubes
¾ cup finely chopped onion
½ teaspoon salt
2 tablespoons shortening
1 can (10½ ounces) condensed beef broth
1 can (10¾ ounces) condensed tomato soup
⅛ teaspoon thyme leaves, crushed
1 can (about 16 ounces) small whole white potatoes, drained and cut up
1 can (about 8 ounces) peas, undrained

Mix *thoroughly* beef, egg, bread cubes, ¼ cup onion, and salt. Shape firmly into 36 meatballs. In large heavy pan, brown meatballs in shortening; pour off fat. Add remaining ingredients. Heat; stir occasionally. Makes about 6½ cups.

PORK LOIN-TO-PERFECTION

3 to 4-pound pork loin rib roast
2 tablespoons shortening
1 can (10¾ ounces) condensed golden mushroom soup
½ cup water
½ cup chopped onion
1 tablespoon paprika
1 medium bay leaf
½ teaspoon salt
Dash pepper
6 medium carrots, cut in 2-inch pieces
4 medium potatoes, cut in half

In large heavy pan, brown meat in shortening; pour off fat. Add soup, water, onion, and seasonings. Cover; cook over low heat 1 hour 15 minutes. Stir occasionally. Add carrots and potatoes. Cook 1 hour more or until done. Remove bay leaf. Thicken sauce if desired. Makes 4 to 6 servings.

DUTCH CHOWDER 'n' DUMPLINGS

1½ cups cooked pork cut in strips
¼ cup chopped onion
2 tablespoons butter or margarine
2 cans (11¼ ounces each) condensed green pea soup
1½ soup cans water
1 package (10 ounces) frozen mixed vegetables, cooked and drained
¼ teaspoon ground nutmeg
Generous dash salt
½ cup biscuit mix
2 teaspoons chopped parsley
3 tablespoons milk

In saucepan, brown pork and cook onion in butter until tender. Add soup; gradually blend in water. Add vegetables, nutmeg, and salt. Bring to boil. Meanwhile, combine biscuit mix, parsley, and milk; drop by teaspoonsful into simmering soup. Cook 5 minutes. Cover; cook 5 minutes more or until done. Makes about 6½ cups.

ORIENTAL BEEF 'n' VEGETABLES

½ pound ground beef
½ cup sliced onion
2 cans (19 ounces each) chunky vegetable soup
1 can (16 ounces) Chinese vegetables, drained
1 tablespoon soy sauce
1 tablespoon cornstarch
Chinese noodles or cooked rice

In saucepan, brown beef and cook onion until tender (use shortening if necessary). Stir to separate meat; pour off fat. Add remaining ingredients except noodles. Cook, stirring until thickened. Serve over Chinese noodles with additional soy. Makes about 6 cups.

PORK LOIN with CARAWAY GRAVY

3-pound boneless rolled loin of pork
Generous dash pepper
1 can (11 ounces) condensed Cheddar cheese soup
1 tablespoon vinegar
1 teaspoon brown sugar
½ teaspoon caraway seed
4 medium carrots (about ½ pound), quartered
1 medium head cabbage, cut in 4 wedges
¼ cup water
2 tablespoons flour

In roasting pan (13x9x2"), place meat fat-side up. Season with pepper. Roast at 325°F. for 1 hour. Pour off all but 2 tablespoons drippings; stir in soup, vinegar, sugar, and caraway. Arrange carrots around meat; top with cabbage. Cover with foil. Roast 2 hours more or until done (total roasting time takes 35 to 40 minutes per pound or 170°F. on meat thermometer). Remove meat and vegetables to serving platter; keep warm. Gradually blend water into flour until smooth. On top of range, in roasting pan, slowly stir flour mixture into sauce. Cook, stirring until thickened. Serve with roast. Makes 6 to 8 servings.

MEXICAN HASH

1 can (about 16 ounces) prepared tamales
2 cans (19 ounces each) chunky beef soup
½ cup sliced ripe olives
1 teaspoon chili powder
1 cup shredded sharp Cheddar cheese

Remove wrappings from tamales; cut in half. In saucepan, combine tamales, soup, olives, and chili. Heat; stir occasionally. Garnish with cheese. Makes about 6 cups.

POTS, PANS, AND PEARLS OF WISDOM: *Did you know that a tight-fitting lid on saucepans and skillets can save you money? With well-covered utensils, less heat escapes into the air, so you can use lower heat settings and shorter cooking times.*

Check the bottoms of your pans. If they are flat, they make firmer contact with surface elements, distributing heat more evenly and efficiently.

CHEESY RAVIOLIOS SOUP

¼ pound hot Italian sausage, cut in 1-inch pieces
¼ cup chopped onion
1 can (11 ounces) Cheddar cheese soup
1 soup can water
1 can (15 ounces) beef raviolios in meat sauce
1 can (about 16 ounces) cut green beans, drained
2 tablespoons diced pimiento

In saucepan, cook sausage until done. Add onion; cook until tender. Pour off fat. Stir in soup; gradually add remaining ingredients. Heat; stir occasionally. Makes about 5½ cups.

CAPE COD KETTLE

1 can (10½ ounces) condensed oyster stew
1 can (10¾ ounces) condensed cream of potato soup
2 soup cans milk
1 can (about 7 ounces) salmon or tuna, drained and flaked
1 can (about 8 ounces) whole kernel corn, undrained
1 tablespoon chopped parsley

In saucepan, combine ingredients. Heat; stir occasionally. Makes about 6½ cups.

SAUSAGE SUPPER SOUP

1 package (8 ounces) brown 'n serve sausage links, sliced
1 can (10¾ ounces) condensed cream of chicken soup
1 soup can water
1 package (10 ounces) frozen mixed vegetables, cooked and drained
1 cup cubed zucchini
¼ teaspoon thyme leaves, crushed

In saucepan, brown sausage; pour off fat. Add remaining ingredients. Cook 10 minutes or until vegetables are tender; stir occasionally. Makes about 5 cups.

HAMBURGER SOUP OLÉ

½ pound ground beef
¼ teaspoon salt
Generous dash pepper
½ cup chopped onion
1 small green pepper, cut in squares
1 large clove garlic, minced
¼ teaspoon oregano leaves, crushed
1 can (11 ounces) condensed Cheddar cheese soup
1 can (11¼ ounces) condensed chili beef soup
1½ soup cans water
1 can (about 8 ounces) whole kernel corn, undrained

Season beef with salt and pepper; shape into 16 meatballs. In large saucepan, brown meatballs and cook onion and green pepper with garlic and oregano until tender (use shortening if necessary). Stir in soups; gradually blend in water. Add corn. Heat; stir occasionally. Makes about 7 cups.

SUNDAY POT ROAST

3 to 4-pound boneless pot roast
1 can (10½ ounces) condensed beef broth
½ teaspoon salt
¼ teaspoon pepper
¼ teaspoon rosemary leaves, crushed
6 small carrots, cut in half lengthwise (about ½ pound)
2 medium yellow turnips, quartered (about 1½ pounds)
8 small whole white onions (about ½ pound)

In large heavy pan, brown meat on all sides (use shortening if necessary); pour off fat. Add soup and seasonings. Cover; cook over low heat 2 hours. Add carrots, turnips, and onions. Cook 1 hour more or until done. Stir occasionally. Remove meat and vegetables to heated platter. Spoon off fat; thicken to desired consistency. Makes 6 to 8 servings.

JUST TIP ME OVER AND POUR ME OUT: *Better to boil water in a tea kettle than to use an open pan. A closed container is faster—and energy-conserving.*

CONFETTI CHICKEN CHOWDER

4 slices bacon
1 can (about 4 ounces) sliced mushrooms, drained
½ cup chopped onion
⅛ teaspoon thyme leaves, crushed
1 can (10¾ ounces) condensed cream of celery soup
1 can (10½ ounces) condensed chicken vegetable soup
1 soup can water
1½ cups diced cooked chicken
1 can (about 8 ounces) whole kernel corn, undrained
½ cup chopped canned tomatoes
Dash pepper

In saucepan, cook bacon until crisp; remove and crumble. Pour off all but 2 tablespoons drippings. Brown mushrooms and cook onion with thyme in drippings until tender. Add remaining ingredients except bacon. Heat; stir occasionally. Garnish with bacon. Makes about 5½ cups.

PIZZA POTAGE

½ pound ground beef
¼ teaspoon onion salt
2 tablespoons shortening
1 can (10½ ounces) condensed old fashioned vegetable soup
1 can (10¾ ounces) condensed tomato soup
1½ soup cans water
1 cup cooked spiral-shaped macaroni
2 tablespoons chopped parsley
¼ teaspoon oregano leaves, crushed
Grated Parmesan cheese

Mix *thoroughly* beef and onion salt; shape into 12 meatballs. In saucepan, brown meatballs in shortening; pour off fat. Add remaining ingredients except cheese. Heat; stir occasionally. Serve with cheese. Makes about 6 cups.

WESTERN CHILI

- **1 pound ground beef**
- **½ cup chopped green pepper**
- **½ cup chopped onion**
- **2 tablespoons chili powder**
- **2 cans (11¼ ounces each) condensed chili beef soup**
- **½ cup water**
- **1 can (16 ounces) tomatoes, cut up**
- **1 can (15½ ounces) kidney beans, undrained**

In large saucepan, brown beef and cook green pepper and onion with chili powder until tender (use shortening if necessary). Stir to separate meat. Add remaining ingredients. Simmer 15 minutes; stir often. Makes about 8 cups.

BEEF BURGUNDY GOULASH

- **1½ pounds beef cubes (1½ inch)**
- **2 tablespoons shortening**
- **2 cans (10½ ounces each) condensed onion soup**
- **½ soup can water**
- **½ soup can Burgundy or other dry red wine**
- **3 cups uncooked medium noodles**
- **1 cup sliced carrots**

In large heavy pan, brown beef in shortening; pour off fat. Add soup, water, and Burgundy. Cover; cook over low heat 2 hours. Add noodles and carrots. Cook 20 minutes more or until done. Stir occasionally. Add additional water if necessary. Makes about 6 cups.

BROWN-BAGGING CAN BE BEAUTIFUL: *For business people and scholars of every description, the carried lunch offers a pennywise alternative to the cafeteria line. Here's a perfect niche for leftovers and a good excuse to put your imagination in high gear.*

For starters, pack soup in vacuum containers. Rinse the vacuum bottle with hot water before pouring in hot soup, cold water for cold soup.

Add a sandwich—or a salad—or fruit and cheese.

AUTUMN BEEF STEW

- 2 pounds beef cubes (1½ inch)
- 2 tablespoons shortening
- 2 cans (10¾ ounces each) condensed golden mushroom or cream of mushroom soup
- ½ cup water
- 1 tablespoon Worcestershire
- 6 medium carrots, cut in 2-inch pieces
- 8 small whole white onions (about ½ pound)
- 1 package (9 ounces) frozen cut green beans
- Cooked noodles

In large heavy pan, brown beef in shortening; pour off fat. Add soup, water, and Worcestershire. Cover; cook over low heat 1 hour 30 minutes. Add carrots and onions. Cook 45 minutes more. Add beans. Cook 15 minutes more or until done. Stir occasionally. Thicken sauce if desired. Serve over noodles. Makes about 7 cups.

OLD-FASHIONED SUPPER SOUP

- ½ cup chopped onion
- 1 medium clove garlic, minced
- 1 teaspoon basil leaves, crushed
- 2 tablespoons butter or margarine
- 2 cans (10¾ ounces each) condensed golden mushroom soup
- 2 soup cans water
- 1 can (about 16 ounces) stewed tomatoes, cut up
- 2 cups diced cooked chicken or turkey
- 1½ cups uncooked medium noodles

In large heavy pan, cook onion and garlic with basil in butter until tender. Stir in soup and water; add remaining ingredients. Bring to boil; reduce heat. Cook 10 minutes or until noodles are done; stir occasionally. Makes about 8 cups.

THE ROAST WITH THE MOST: *When comparing the cost of similar foods, especially meat, consider cost per serving rather than cost per pound or total cost.*

A boneless roast, for instance, is often more economical than a cheaper per-pound cut with bone, simply because you wind up with more servings.

CHUCK STEAK and VEGETABLES

4 medium carrots (about ½ pound), halved lengthwise
2-pound boneless chuck steak (1-inch thick), well trimmed
2 tablespoons shortening
Dash salt
Dash paprika
Dash pepper
1 can (10½ ounces) condensed onion soup
3 medium potatoes (about 1 pound), quartered

Cut carrots into 3-inch pieces. In large heavy pan, brown steak in shortening; pour off fat. Season with salt, paprika, and pepper. Add soup. Cover; cook over low heat 45 minutes. Add carrots and potatoes. Cook 45 minutes more or until done. Stir occasionally. Spoon off fat; thicken sauce if desired. Makes 4 servings.

KENTUCKY CHICKEN CHOWDER

1 cup chopped onion
¼ teaspoon basil leaves, crushed
¼ teaspoon thyme leaves, crushed
2 tablespoons butter or margarine
2 cans (10¾ ounces each) condensed chicken broth
2 cups shredded raw potato
1½ cups cubed cooked chicken
1 package (10 ounces) frozen succotash
1 can (about 8 ounces) tomatoes, cut up
1 soup can water
⅛ teaspoon pepper

In large saucepan, cook onion with basil and thyme in butter until tender. Add remaining ingredients. Bring to boil; reduce heat. Cover; simmer 20 minutes or until vegetables are done. Stir often. Makes about 8 cups.

BAYOU FISH STEW

½ cup sliced onion
2 tablespoons butter or margarine
1 can (10¾ ounces) condensed cream of chicken soup
¼ cup water
1 pound fillets of white fish, cut up
1 package (10 ounces) frozen whole okra
1 large bay leaf
¼ teaspoon salt
1 medium tomato, cut in wedges

In skillet, cook onion in butter until tender. Add remaining ingredients except tomato. Bring to boil; stir to separate okra. Reduce heat. Simmer 15 minutes or until done. Stir occasionally. Add tomatoes; heat. Remove bay leaf. Makes about 4½ cups.

FRANKFURTER CREOLE CHOWDER

1 pound frankfurters, cut in ½-inch slices
¼ teaspoon basil or thyme leaves, crushed
2 tablespoons butter or margarine
1 can (11½ ounces) condensed split pea with ham soup
1 can (10¾ ounces) condensed cream of potato soup
½ soup can water
1 can (about 8 ounces) tomatoes, cut up
1 can (about 8 ounces) whole kernel corn, undrained

In large saucepan, brown frankfurters with basil in butter. Add soups; gradually stir in water. Add remaining ingredients. Heat; stir occasionally. Makes about 6 cups.

THE BIG BIRD OF HAPPINESS: *When it comes to buying turkey and chicken, think big and save. The larger the bird, the more meat and less bone and fat per pound. What's more, leftovers can be transformed into delicious main dishes like DEEP DISH TURKEY PIE (page 7).*

Do make sure your oven and refrigerator can hold these heavyweights, however.

soup mates

Team up two different soups in a saucepan and you've got something to cheer about.

ONE SOUP + SECOND SOUP + LIQUID = SOUP MATE

Simply heat and stir.

ONE SOUP	SECOND SOUP	LIQUID
BEAN WITH BACON	BEEF	1½ SOUP CANS WATER
BEEF	VEGETABLE BEEF	1½ SOUP CANS WATER
BEEF BROTH	TOMATO	1½ SOUP CANS WATER
CREAM OF CELERY	GREEN PEA	1½ SOUP CANS WATER
CHEDDAR CHEESE	TOMATO BISQUE	2 SOUP CANS WATER
CHICKEN 'N DUMPLINGS	CHICKEN VEGETABLE	1½ SOUP CANS WATER
CHICKEN GUMBO	MANHATTAN STYLE CLAM CHOWDER	1½ SOUP CANS WATER
CHICKEN GUMBO	CHICKEN NOODLE-O'S	1½ SOUP CANS WATER
CHICKEN GUMBO	VEGETABLE	1½ SOUP CANS WATER
CHICKEN NOODLE	CHICKEN & STARS	1½ SOUP CANS WATER
CHICKEN VEGETABLE	GOLDEN VEGETABLE NOODLE-O'S	1½ SOUP CANS WATER
CHILI BEEF	VEGETABLE BEEF	1½ SOUP CANS WATER
GOLDEN MUSHROOM	NOODLES & GROUND BEEF	1½ SOUP CANS WATER
GOLDEN MUSHROOM	STOCKPOT	1½ SOUP CANS WATER
CREAM OF MUSHROOM	CREAM OF SHRIMP	1 SOUP CAN MILK 1 SOUP CAN WATER
NOODLES & GROUND BEEF	TOMATO RICE	1½ SOUP CANS WATER
ONION	STOCKPOT	1½ SOUP CANS WATER
PEPPER POT	VEGETABLE BEEF	1½ SOUP CANS WATER
SPLIT PEA WITH HAM	TOMATO	1 SOUP CAN MILK 1 SOUP CAN WATER

cooking big

Come one, come all . . . and bring your appetites. Bill of fare: A few good dishes and plenty of each. Here's a batch of crowd-pleasers you can whip together almost effortlessly—18 tasty ways to say, "*Come again*".

HOMESTYLE CHICKEN SKILLET

4 pounds chicken parts
4 tablespoons shortening
2 cans (11 ounces each) condensed Cheddar cheese soup
4 teaspoons salt
¼ teaspoon pepper
1 teaspoon poultry seasoning
2 cups raw regular rice
2 soup cans water
2 cups chopped canned tomatoes
2 packages (9 ounces each) frozen Italian green beans

Prepare in 2 skillets (10″ each) by dividing ingredients equally. Brown chicken in shortening; pour off fat. Add soup and seasonings. Cover; cook over low heat 15 minutes. Add rice, water, tomatoes, and beans. Bring to boil; stir to separate beans. Reduce heat. Cook covered 30 minutes more or until rice is done. Stir often. Makes 8 servings.

A TIME TO THAW: *When the frost in your freezer gets about ¼ inch thick, defrost. You'll be doing your utility bill a favor since frost makes your freezer work harder to keep the same temperature.*

YANKEE CHILI

1½ pounds ground beef
1 cup chopped onion
2 medium cloves garlic, minced
1 can (10½ ounces) condensed beef broth
2 cans (10¾ ounces each) condensed tomato soup
1 soup can water
2 cans (15½ ounces each) kidney beans, undrained
3 cups cooked elbow macaroni
3 tablespoons chili powder
2 tablespoons vinegar

In large saucepan, brown beef and cook onion with garlic until tender (use shortening if necessary). Stir to separate meat. Add remaining ingredients. Simmer 30 minutes; stir occasionally. Makes about 12 cups.

ROMAN CASSEROLE

1 pound ground beef
½ pound hot Italian sausage, cut in ½-inch slices
1 cup chopped onion
2 teaspoons oregano leaves, crushed
1 can (11 ounces) condensed Cheddar cheese soup
1 can (10¾ ounces) condensed tomato soup
1 cup water
4 cups cooked wide noodles
4 slices (about 4 ounces) Cheddar cheese, cut in half diagonally

In skillet, brown beef and cook sausage and onion with oregano until done (use shortening if necessary); stir to separate meat. Pour off fat. Add soups, water, and noodles; pour into 2-quart shallow baking dish (12x8x2"). Cover; bake at 400°F. for 40 minutes or until hot. Uncover; stir. Top with cheese; bake until cheese melts. Makes about 8 cups.

STOVE-TOP MACARONI and CHEESE

1 cup chopped onion
4 tablespoons butter or margarine
2 cans (10¾ ounces each) condensed cream of chicken soup
1½ cups water
1 tablespoon Worcestershire
⅛ teaspoon pepper
6 cups cooked elbow macaroni
4 cups shredded sharp Cheddar cheese (about 1 pound)
1 package (10 ounces) frozen mixed vegetables, cooked and drained

In large heavy pan, cook onion in butter until tender. Add soup; gradually blend in water. Stir in remaining ingredients. Heat until cheese melts; stir often. Makes about 10½ cups.

HAM 'n' POTATOES HAWAIIAN

1 can (about 8 ounces) pineapple slices in unsweetened juice
3 cups cooked ham cut in strips
6 tablespoons butter or margarine
6 cups cubed cooked potatoes
1 cup chopped onion
½ cup coarsely chopped green pepper
¼ teaspoon thyme leaves, crushed
2 cans (10¾ ounces each) condensed cream of mushroom soup
1 tablespoon Worcestershire
⅛ teaspoon pepper
Green pepper rings

Drain pineapple, reserving juice. In large skillet or heavy pan, brown ham in 2 tablespoons butter; remove. In same skillet, brown potatoes and cook onion and chopped green pepper with thyme in 4 tablespoons butter until tender. Stir in ham, soup, reserved juice, Worcestershire, and pepper. Add potato mixture. Heat; stir occasionally. Garnish with pineapple slices and green pepper rings. Makes about 10 cups.

AU GRATIN FRANKS 'n' POTATOES

6 cups cubed raw potatoes
1 cup diced green pepper
1 cup chopped onion
4 tablespoons butter or margarine
1 teaspoon salt
¼ teaspoon pepper
1½ pounds frankfurters, diagonally sliced
1 can (11 ounces) condensed Cheddar cheese soup
1 package (3 ounces) cream cheese, softened
½ cup water
¼ cup ketchup

In covered large heavy pan, cook potatoes, green pepper, and onion in 3 tablespoons butter until potatoes are *just* tender (about 20 minutes). Stir occasionally. Season with salt and pepper. Push potatoes to the side; add frankfurters and remaining 1 tablespoon butter; brown. In bowl, gradually blend soup into cream cheese until smooth; add water and ketchup. Stir into potato-frankfurter mixture. Heat; stir occasionally. Makes about 9 cups.

OVEN-BARBECUED SPARERIBS

8 pounds spareribs, cut in serving-size pieces
2 cans (10½ ounces each) condensed onion soup
1 cup chili sauce
¼ cup dry mustard
¼ cup steak sauce
2 tablespoons brown sugar
1 tablespoon vinegar
4 teaspoons cornstarch
1 medium clove garlic, minced

In large heavy pan, cover spareribs with water. Simmer 1 hour; drain. Arrange in single layer in two 2½-quart shallow baking dishes (13x9x2"). Meanwhile, in saucepan, combine remaining ingredients. Cook over low heat 5 minutes; stir often. Spoon on ribs. Bake at 325°F. for 1 hour or until done. Makes 8 servings.

SOUPERBURGER

4 pounds ground beef
2 cups chopped onion
2 tablespoons salad oil
4 cans (10¾ ounces each) condensed cream of mushroom soup
3 tablespoons prepared mustard
⅛ teaspoon pepper
Toasted hamburger buns

In large heavy pan, brown beef and cook onion in oil until tender. Stir to separate meat; pour off fat. Stir in soup, mustard, and pepper. Heat; stir occasionally. Serve over buns. Makes about 12 cups.

A KNACK FOR SNACKING: *If your family is dedicated to between-meal munching, make the most of it, nutritionwise. Offer them foods that fit right in with the day's meal plans—fresh fruits and vegetables, hot soups, juices, milk shakes, ice cream, cheese, nuts, oatmeal cookies. In other words, foods that take up where your menu plans leave off to provide servings from the Four Food Groups.*

Meanwhile, banish snacks that offer calories only. You'll be surprised at the savings—with absolutely no sacrifice in nutrients.

NOODLEBURGER SCALLOP

2 pounds ground beef
½ cup chopped celery
2 medium cloves garlic, minced
1 teaspoon salt
⅛ teaspoon pepper
1 can (11 ounces) condensed Cheddar cheese soup
1 can (10¾ ounces) condensed cream of mushroom soup
⅔ cup milk
½ cup sour cream
4 cups cooked noodles
4 tomato slices, halved
Shredded process cheese

In skillet, brown beef and cook celery with garlic until tender. Pour off fat. Add salt and pepper. In large bowl, blend soups, milk, and sour cream. In two 1½-quart casseroles, layer noodles, meat, and soup mixture. Bake at 400°F. for 25 minutes; stir. Top with tomato and cheese. Bake until cheese melts. Makes 8 servings.

JUMBO TUNA GUMBO

2 cans (10¾ ounces each) condensed chicken gumbo soup
2 soup cans milk
2 cans (about 7 ounces each) tuna, drained and flaked
1 can (about 16 ounces) cream style corn
2 cups cubed cooked potatoes
⅛ teaspoon pepper

In saucepan, combine ingredients. Heat; stir occasionally. Makes about 9½ cups.

***IN SEARCH OF THE PERFECT PARTY FOOD** . . . easy, economical, enticing. That's cheese. What could be handier than putting together a tray of fruit, bread, crackers, and a variety of cheeses?*

Here's hidden economy, too: No waste. Just refrigerate what is left in airtight containers for future use.

As for enjoyment, you can enhance yours by removing cheese (still covered) from the refrigerator a little while before serving. Almost any cheese, except cream cheese, tastes better this way.

CHICKEN MAJORCA

4 whole chicken breasts (about 3 pounds), split
¼ cup shortening
1 can (11 ounces) condensed Cheddar cheese soup
1 can (10¾ ounces) condensed cream of chicken soup
1 can (about 4 ounces) sliced mushrooms, drained
2 tablespoons chopped pimiento
½ teaspoon thyme leaves, crushed
2 packages (10 ounces each) frozen cut asparagus

Use 1 large skillet or prepare in 2 skillets (about 10″ each) by dividing ingredients equally. Brown chicken in shortening; pour off fat. Stir in soups, mushrooms, pimiento, and thyme; add asparagus. Cover; cook over low heat 30 minutes or until done. Stir occasionally. Makes 8 servings.

CHICKEN NOODLE SCALLOP

2 cans (10¾ ounces each) condensed cream of chicken soup
¾ cup sour cream
4 cups cooked noodles
3 cups cubed cooked chicken
2 cups cooked peas
1 teaspoon salt
¼ teaspoon pepper
¼ teaspoon rubbed sage

In large heavy pan, blend soup and sour cream. Add remaining ingredients. Heat; stir occasionally. Makes about 10 cups.

Dutch Chowder 'n' Dumplings—recipe page 84

BAKED SPAGHETTI

2 pounds ground beef
½ pound hot Italian sausage, sliced
1½ cups chopped onion
2 large cloves garlic, minced
1 tablespoon Italian seasoning, crushed
4 cans (10¾ ounces each) condensed tomato soup
3 soup cans water
1 tablespoon vinegar
2 teaspoons salt
1 pound spaghetti, cooked and drained
Grated Parmesan cheese

In large heavy pan, brown beef and cook sausage and onion with garlic and Italian seasoning until done. Stir to separate meat. Stir in soup, water, vinegar, and salt. Simmer 15 minutes; stir occasionally. Add spaghetti. Transfer to two 2½-quart shallow baking dishes (13x9x2″). Bake at 400°F. for 30 minutes or until hot; stir. Top with cheese. Makes about 15 cups.

CANDLELIGHT CHICKEN

1 jar (about 2½ ounces) sliced dried beef, rinsed and drained
4 whole chicken breasts, split, skinned, and boned (about 2 pounds boneless)
2 cans (10¾ ounces each) condensed cream of mushroom soup
1 cup sour cream
6 slices bacon, cut in half
Cooked rice

In 2½-quart shallow baking dish (13x9x2″), arrange single layer of beef; top with chicken. Blend soup and sour cream; pour over all. Top with bacon. Bake at 400°F. for 1 hour or until done. Serve with rice. Makes 8 servings.

Autumn Beef Stew—recipe page 90

GOLD RUSH CHICKEN

5 pounds chicken parts
¼ cup melted butter or margarine
3 cans (10¾ ounces each) condensed golden mushroom soup
½ cup sweet vermouth or grape juice
½ cup chopped parsley
½ teaspoon poultry seasoning

In two 2-quart shallow baking dishes (12x8x2″), arrange chicken in a single layer skin-side up; brush with butter. Bake at 400°F. for 45 minutes; baste once with pan drippings. Combine remaining ingredients; spoon over chicken. Bake 15 minutes more or until done. Makes 10 servings.

SCALLOPED POTATOES PARMESAN

2 cans (11 ounces each) condensed Cheddar cheese soup
½ cup milk
¼ cup grated Parmesan cheese
8 cups thinly sliced potatoes
1 cup thinly sliced onion
1 tablespoon butter or margarine
Paprika

In bowl, blend soup, milk, and Parmesan. In buttered 3-quart shallow baking dish (13x9x2″), arrange alternate layers of potatoes, onion, and sauce. Dot top with butter; sprinkle with paprika. Cover; bake at 400°F. for 45 minutes. Uncover; bake 15 minutes more or until potatoes are tender. Makes about 7½ cups.

DON'T SNUB THE SPUD: *Eat the whole thing. If you eagerly devour the tender insides of a baked potato—but not the skin—you're leaving a lot behind. Vitamins are concentrated near the skin, and the skin itself provides valuable roughage to aid digestion.*

STUFFED TURKEY

6 slices bacon
1 cup sliced celery
½ cup chopped onion
1 package (8½ ounces) herb-seasoned stuffing mix
2 cups coarse cornbread crumbs
1 can (10½ ounces) condensed beef broth
1 egg, slightly beaten
10-pound turkey
1 can (10¾ ounces) condensed cream of mushroom soup
½ cup whole berry cranberry sauce
¼ cup orange juice

In skillet, cook bacon until crisp; remove and crumble. Pour off all but 2 tablespoons drippings. Cook celery and onion in drippings until tender. Toss lightly with stuffing mix, cornbread, broth, and egg. Fill cavity of turkey loosely with stuffing. Truss; place in roasting pan. Cover with foil. Roast at 325°F. for about 4 hours (25 minutes per pound or until tender). Uncover last hour to brown. Remove turkey to serving platter. Skim fat from drippings; add remaining ingredients. Heat; stir to loosen browned bits. Makes 12 servings.

SPEEDY TETRAZZINI

1 cup thinly sliced celery
4 tablespoons butter or margarine
3 cans (10¾ ounces each) condensed Cheddar cheese soup
1 can (16 ounces) tomatoes, chopped
5 cups cooked spaghetti
3 cans (about 7 ounces each) tuna, drained and flaked

In large heavy pan, cook celery in butter until tender. Stir in soup. Add remaining ingredients. Heat; stir occasionally. Makes about 9 cups.

et cetera

Appetizers, desserts, vegetables, breads, salads, dressings, sandwiches, beverages—all the little things that mean a lot to your menus are included in this section. Each is a small treasure guaranteed to brighten any table, pamper every palate . . . again and again.

CHILI SHRIMP DIP

1 can (10¾ ounces) condensed cream of shrimp soup
1 package (8 ounces) cream cheese, softened
¼ cup finely chopped celery
2 tablespoons chili sauce
1 tablespoon finely chopped onion
Dash Worcestershire

With electric mixer or rotary beater, gradually blend soup into cream cheese. Beat *just* until smooth (overbeating makes dip thin). Stir in remaining ingredients. Chill 4 hours or more. Serve as a dip with crackers or chips. Makes about 2 cups.

ZIPPY CLAM DIP

1 can (10¾ ounces) condensed cream of celery soup
1 package (8 ounces) cream cheese, softened
1 can (8 ounces) minced clams, well-drained
1 tablespoon chopped parsley
2 teaspoons prepared horseradish

With electric mixer or rotary beater, gradually blend soup into cream cheese. Beat *just* until smooth (overbeating makes dip thin). Stir in remaining ingredients. Chill. Serve as a dip with crackers or chips. Makes about 2½ cups.

CACTUS CORN

4 slices bacon
¼ cup green pepper strips
1 can (11 ounces) condensed Cheddar cheese soup
3 cups cooked whole kernel corn
½ cup drained chopped canned tomatoes

In saucepan, cook bacon until crisp; remove and crumble. Pour off all but 2 tablespoons drippings. Cook green pepper in drippings until tender. Add soup, corn, and tomatoes. Heat; stir occasionally. Garnish with bacon. Makes about 4 cups.

CARAWAY CHEESE BREAD

6½ to 7 cups sifted all-purpose flour
2 packages active dry yeast
¼ cup grated Parmesan cheese
1 tablespoon caraway seed
1 can (11 ounces) condensed Cheddar cheese soup
1½ cups water
3 tablespoons butter or margarine
3 tablespoons sugar
2 teaspoons salt

In large bowl, combine 3 cups flour, yeast, cheese, and caraway. In saucepan, heat remaining ingredients to lukewarm; add to dry ingredients. Beat at low speed of electric mixer 30 seconds, scraping sides of bowl. Beat at high speed 3 minutes. Stir in enough remaining flour to make a stiff dough. Knead until smooth on lightly floured board (about 10 minutes). Place in greased bowl, turning once. Cover; let rise in warm place until doubled (about 1 hour). Punch down. Cover; let rest 10 minutes. Divide dough in half. Shape each half into a loaf. Place each in a greased loaf pan (9x5x3"). Cover; let rise until doubled (about 1 hour). Bake at 400°F. for 30 minutes or until done. Makes 2 loaves.

JACK FROST BEAN BAKE

4 slices bacon
1 cup sliced onion
1 can (10¾ ounces) condensed cream of mushroom soup
¼ cup chili sauce
1 teaspoon Worcestershire
⅛ teaspoon hot pepper sauce
2 packages (10 ounces each) frozen lima beans, cooked and drained
½ cup shredded Cheddar cheese

In saucepan, cook bacon until crisp; remove and crumble. Pour off all but 2 tablespoons drippings. Cook onion in drippings until tender. Stir in soup, chili sauce, Worcestershire, and hot pepper sauce. Add beans and bacon. Pour into 1½-quart casserole. Bake at 400°F. for 25 minutes or until hot; stir. Top with cheese; bake until cheese melts. Makes about 5 cups.

DANISH PASTRIES

2 packages (14 to 18 ounces each) hot roll mix
1 can (11 ounces) condensed Cheddar cheese soup
2 eggs, slightly beaten
½ cup sugar
½ teaspoon almond extract

In large bowl, dissolve yeast from both boxes of mix as directed using *only* ¾ cup water. Follow mix directions adding *undiluted* soup, eggs, sugar, and extract with flour mixture. Let rise as directed. Shape dough into 48 small balls; flatten to form 1½-inch circles. Place on lightly greased cookie sheets; let rise again until doubled. Press center of each circle to make indentation; spoon about 1 tablespoon filling* in each. Bake at 375°F. for 20 minutes or until brown. Cool; glaze if desired. Makes 48 pastries.

**Fillings:* Assorted prepared fruit pie fillings or pineapple cream cheese.

To Make Ahead: Freeze baked pastries in single layer; wrap in freezer wrap.

MEXICALI TACOS

2 pounds ground beef
½ cup chopped green pepper
1 can (11¼ ounces) condensed chili beef soup
1 can (10¾ ounces) condensed tomato soup
1 to 2 tablespoons finely chopped cherry peppers
24 taco shells
Shredded Cheddar or Monterey Jack cheese
Shredded lettuce
Chopped onion
Diced tomato

In skillet, brown beef and cook green pepper until tender; stir to separate meat. Add soups and cherry peppers. Cook over low heat 5 minutes; stir occasionally. Fill each taco shell with 3 to 4 tablespoons meat mixture; top each with remaining ingredients. Makes 24 tacos.

CHEESECAKE PIE

Crumb Crust:

2 cups fine vanilla wafer or graham cracker crumbs
6 tablespoons butter or margarine, melted
¼ cup sugar

Filling:

12 ounces cream cheese, softened
⅔ cup sugar
3 eggs
1 can (11 ounces) condensed Cheddar cheese soup
2 tablespoons lemon juice
1 teaspoon grated lemon rind
1 teaspoon vanilla extract
¼ teaspoon almond extract

Topping:

1 cup sour cream
¼ cup sugar
1 teaspoon grated lemon rind
1 teaspoon vanilla extract

Crust: Combine crumbs, butter, and sugar. Press firmly into 10" pie plate. Chill.

Filling: With electric mixer, beat cream cheese until smooth. Add sugar and eggs alternately. Blend in *1 cup* soup, lemon juice, rind, and flavorings. Pour into chilled pie crust. Bake at 350°F. for 50 minutes.

Topping: Blend sour cream, remaining soup, sugar, lemon rind, and vanilla. Spread on pie. Bake 5 minutes more. Cool; chill. Top with prepared fruit pie filling.

THERE'S MORE TO DESSERT THAN A HAPPY SWEET TOOTH: *Stop thinking of dessert as a mere frill. Instead, make it an integral part of every meal plan and reap more nutrition for your money.*

Has the day been low in fruits and vegetables? Baked apple dessert to the rescue. Need another serving of milk to round out the family's intake? Let them eat custard for the grand finale. You get the idea—and that sweet tooth needn't suffer a bit.

SEAFOOD DRESSING

1 can (10¾ ounces) condensed cream of shrimp soup
1 cup mayonnaise
2 chopped hard-cooked eggs
¼ cup chili sauce
¼ cup chopped green pepper
2 tablespoons finely chopped onion
1 teaspoon lemon juice

In bowl, combine ingredients. Serve over crisp salad greens or seafood. Makes about 3 cups.

DILL-SPIKED ONION ROLLS

2 packages (14 to 18 ounces each) hot roll mix
1 can (10¾ ounces) condensed cream of onion soup
2 eggs, slightly beaten
½ cup grated Parmesan cheese
1 tablespoon dried dill weed

In large bowl, dissolve yeast from both boxes of mix as directed using *only* ¾ cup water. Follow mix directions adding *undiluted* soup, eggs, cheese, and dill with flour mixture. Let rise as directed. Shape dough into 16 large or 32 small rolls. Place on lightly greased cookie sheets; let rise again until doubled. Bake at 375°F. for 20 minutes or until brown. Makes 16 large or 32 small rolls.

PLAY IT AGAIN, CHEF: *Leftover vegetables? Don't send last night's green beans, carrots, peas, cauliflower, broccoli to Never-Never Land. Add them to tonight's salad greens for a peppy change. Top with grated Parmesan cheese, onion rings, or croutons.*

Leftover meat or poultry? Team them with a little cheese and sliced hard-cooked eggs, to transform ordinary salad greens into a luscious main dish Chef's Salad.

TWICE-BAKED POTATOES

8 medium baking potatoes
2 tablespoons butter or margarine
¼ teaspoon salt
1 can (11 ounces) condensed Cheddar cheese soup
1 tablespoon chopped dried chives
Paprika

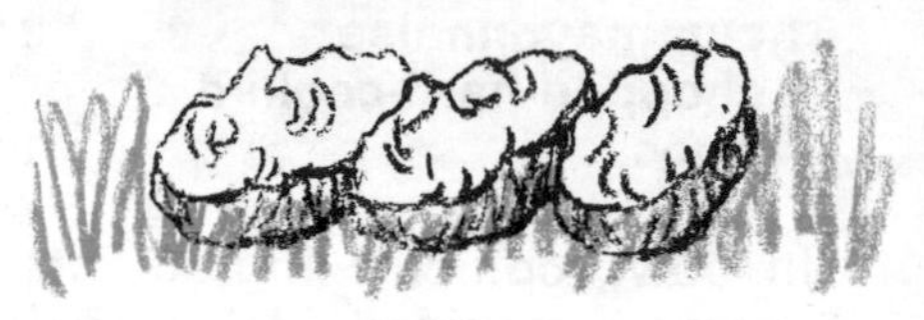

Bake potatoes until done. Cut potatoes in half lengthwise; scoop out insides leaving a thin shell. With electric mixer, mash potatoes with butter and salt. Gradually add soup and chives; beat until light and fluffy. Spoon into shells. Sprinkle with paprika. Bake in 2½-quart shallow baking dish (13x9x2″) at 450°F. for 15 minutes or until hot. Makes 8 servings.

SOUTH-of-the-BORDER DIP

1 can (11 ounces) condensed black bean soup
1 package (3 ounces) cream cheese, softened
⅓ cup chopped canned tomatoes
¼ cup finely chopped onion
1 tablespoon chopped hot cherry peppers
2 teaspoons chili powder

With electric mixer or rotary beater, gradually blend soup into cream cheese. Beat *just* until smooth (overbeating makes dip thin). Stir in remaining ingredients. Chill 4 hours or more. Serve as a dip with crackers or chips. Makes about 2 cups.

***OPERATION CORNUCOPIA:** Fresh fruits and vegetables are most plentiful—and priced attractively—in season. That's when to enjoy them for all they're worth.*

APPLE CRISP

1 can (11 ounces) condensed Cheddar cheese soup
1 cup packed brown sugar
1 teaspoon lemon juice
1 teaspoon ground cinnamon
½ teaspoon ground nutmeg
8 cups very thinly sliced apples (about 8 apples)
¾ cup quick-cooking oats, uncooked
¼ cup chopped walnuts
2 tablespoons milk
1 tablespoon butter or margarine, softened

Combine soup, ¼ cup sugar, lemon juice, cinnamon, and nutmeg. Toss apples with soup mixture; pour into buttered 8″ square or 10″ round baking dish. Combine ¾ cup sugar with remaining ingredients; sprinkle over apples. Bake at 375°F. for 45 minutes or until apples are tender. Allow to stand 15 minutes or more before serving. Serve with a whipped topping or ice cream if desired. Makes about 5½ cups.

CHEESE DIVAN

2 packages (10 ounces each) frozen broccoli spears, cooked and drained
1 can (11 ounces) condensed Cheddar cheese soup
¼ cup sour cream
2 tablespoons milk
1 can (about 8 ounces) whole kernel corn, drained
¼ teaspoon curry powder

In 1½-quart shallow baking dish (10x6x2″), arrange broccoli. Blend soup, sour cream, milk, corn, and curry; pour over broccoli. Bake at 400°F. for 20 minutes or until hot. Garnish with pimiento if desired. Makes 4 to 6 servings.

DON'T THROW IT TO THE BIRDS: *Instead, dry stale bread slices in a slow oven. Crush for bread crumbs. Cube before drying for croutons to pep up soups and salads.*

CHEESY SCALLOPED POTATOES

1 can (10¾ ounces) condensed cream of mushroom or celery soup
½ cup milk
Dash pepper
4 cups thinly sliced potatoes
½ cup thinly sliced onion
1 cup shredded sharp Cheddar cheese
1 tablespoon butter or margarine
Dash paprika

Blend soup, milk, and pepper. In 1½-quart casserole, arrange alternate layers of potatoes, onion, sauce, and cheese. Dot top with butter; sprinkle with paprika. Cover; bake at 375°F. for 1 hour. Uncover; bake 15 minutes more or until done. Makes about 4 cups.

WHICH CUPBOARD, MOTHER HUBBARD? *There are some kitchen cabinets that* ***should*** *be bare—of food anyway. Those over the range, near the dishwasher, or by the refrigerator exhaust are too warm for food. Store dishes or pans in these places and save the cooler spots for canned goods and staples to insure longer shelf life.*

TOMATO FRENCH DRESSING

1 can (10¾ ounces) condensed tomato soup
¼ cup vinegar
½ cup salad oil
1 tablespoon finely chopped onion
2 tablespoons sugar
2 teaspoons dry mustard
1 teaspoon salt
¼ teaspoon pepper

In covered jar or shaker, combine ingredients. Shake well before using. Serve on crisp salad greens. Makes about 2 cups.

DUAL CHEESE LOGS
(Basic Mixture)

1 can (11½ ounces) condensed bean with bacon soup
4 cups (1 pound) shredded sharp Cheddar cheese
½ cup finely chopped onion

In large bowl of electric mixer, beat ingredients until *smooth*. Divide mixture in half.

Spicy Nut Log:
Stir into ½ of basic mixture:

1 tablespoon Worcestershire
1 small clove garlic, minced
¼ teaspoon hot pepper sauce

Chill. On waxed paper, shape mixture into log (8x1½"); roll in chopped walnuts. Refrigerate.

Taco Cheese Log:
Stir into ½ of basic mixture:

¼ cup taco sauce

Proceed as above for shaping log. Roll in chopped parsley. Refrigerate.

Serve as a spread for breads or crackers. Makes 2 logs.

RHAPSODY IN GREEN: *Salads—cool, crisp, carefree—have saved many a meal from the clutches of monotony. Yet salads themselves can become cliches when the same greens are used over and over.*

Climb out of that iceberg lettuce rut. Brighten your table with romaine, escarole, endive, chicory, watercress, raw spinach, celery tops. The darker the greens, the higher the vitamin and mineral content—and the more nutrition for your money.

Wash greens thoroughly, drain well, roll in paper towels, crisp in refrigerator. In the interest of freshness, make salads at the very last minute. Drooping greens? Perk them up in ice water.

STEAMED PUDDING

- 2½ cups sifted all-purpose flour
- 1 tablespoon baking powder
- ½ teaspoon baking soda
- 1 teaspoon ground cinnamon
- ½ teaspoon ground nutmeg
- 2 cups chopped dates
- ¼ cup shortening
- 1 cup sugar
- 1 egg
- 1 can (10¾ ounces) condensed tomato soup

Sift flour with baking powder, soda, and spices; dust dates with small amount of flour mixture. In bowl, cream shortening and sugar; add egg and mix well. Add dry ingredients alternately with soup; stir well after each addition. Fold in dates. Pour into greased 2-quart mold; cover securely with foil. Place on trivet in large pan. Add boiling water to one-half height of mold. Cover; steam 3 hours. Remove mold from water; uncover and loosen edges of pudding with knife. Unmold while hot. Makes 12 servings.

TRATTORIA GREEN BEANS

- 4 slices bacon
- 1 cup sliced onion
- 2 medium cloves garlic, minced
- 1 teaspoon oregano leaves, crushed
- ¼ teaspoon basil leaves, crushed
- 1 can (10¾ ounces) condensed tomato soup
- ¼ cup water
- 2 packages (9 ounces each) frozen cut green beans
- Grated Parmesan cheese

In skillet, cook bacon until crisp; remove and crumble. Pour off all but 2 tablespoons drippings. Cook onion with garlic, oregano, and basil in drippings until tender. Add soup, water, and beans. Cover; cook over low heat 20 minutes or until beans are tender. Stir occasionally. Garnish with bacon and cheese. Makes about 3½ cups.

Campbell's and Swanson help me make it extra special.

CAMPBELL'S® GREEN BEAN CASSEROLE
Prep Time: 10 min. Cook Time: 30 min.

1 can (10 3/4 oz.) **Campbell's**® Cream of Mushroom **or** 98% Fat Free Cream of Mushroom Soup
1/2 cup milk
1 tsp. soy sauce
Dash pepper
4 cups cooked cut green beans
1 1/3 cups French's® French Fried Onions

dill weed

MIX soup, milk, soy, pepper, beans and **2/3 cup** onions in 1 1/2-qt. casserole.

BAKE at 350°F. for 25 min. or until hot.

STIR. Sprinkle with remaining onions. Bake 5 min. Serves 6.

They love it
toasted nuts!

There's nothing better
than a holiday meal
to bring the family together.

News flash!
The kids ate their
vegetables.

APPLESAUCE OATMEAL COOKIES

2 cups all-purpose flour
1½ teaspoons baking powder
½ teaspoon baking soda
2 teaspoons ground allspice
1 teaspoon ground cinnamon
⅛ teaspoon ground cloves
1 can (11 ounces) condensed Cheddar cheese soup
1½ cups packed brown sugar
1 cup applesauce
1 cup shortening
2 eggs
2 cups quick-cooking oats, uncooked
1 cup seedless raisins
1 cup chopped walnuts

Sift flour, baking powder, baking soda, and spices into large bowl. Add soup, sugar, applesauce, shortening, and eggs. Using electric mixer, beat at medium speed for 2 minutes (300 strokes with spoon), scraping sides and bottom of bowl constantly. Stir in oats, raisins, and nuts. Drop rounded teaspoonfuls on ungreased cookie sheet. Bake at 350°F. for 15 minutes or until lightly browned. Makes about 7½ dozen cookies.

GREEN BEAN BAKE

1 can (10¾ ounces) condensed cream of mushroom soup
½ cup milk
1 teaspoon soy sauce
Dash pepper
2 packages (9 ounces each) frozen green beans, cooked and drained
1 can (3½ ounces) French fried onions

In 1½-quart casserole, combine soup, milk, soy, and pepper; stir in green beans and ½ can onions. Bake at 350°F. for 30 minutes or until hot; stir. Top with remaining onions. Bake 5 minutes more. Makes about 4 cups.

HELP WIPE OUT CELERY SLUMP: *Revive limp celery by placing it in a deep container of water in the refrigerator.*

TOMATO SPICE CAKE MIX

1 package (2 layer) spice cake mix
1 can (10¾ ounces) condensed tomato soup
½ cup water
2 eggs

Mix *only* above ingredients; following directions on package. If desired, fold in 1 cup chopped walnuts. Bake as directed. Frost with your favorite white frosting.

FRUIT CAKE: After mixing, fold in 1 cup chopped candied fruit and 1 cup chopped walnuts. Bake as directed on package adding about 5 minutes more.

MR. MAC GREGOR'S GARDEN: *Vegetables aren't just for rabbits, you know. When prepared with care and served with flair, they're food for the gods at prices most mortals can afford.*

Some friendly advice: Help stamp out overcook. Serve vegetables when ***just tender.*** *Cook in a small amount of water for the shortest time possible. You'll be saving energy as well as flavor, texture, and nutrients.*

ESPAGNOLE SAUCE

1 slice bacon
⅓ cup chopped onion
1 small bay leaf
⅛ teaspoon thyme leaves, crushed
1 can (10¾ ounces) condensed golden mushroom soup
⅓ cup tomato juice
⅓ cup water

In saucepan, cook bacon until crisp; remove and crumble. Cook onion with bay and thyme in drippings until tender. Stir in remaining ingredients. Heat; stir occasionally. Serve over cooked meats, poultry, or vegetables. Makes about 2 cups.

WHAT THE WELL-DRESSED FOOD ITEM WEARS TO THE FREEZER: *Moisture/vapor-proof materials are a must—aluminum foil, polyethylene bags and wraps, freezer film wraps, plastic and metal containers.*

Why is it so important to keep air and moisture out? Because they cause freezer burn which robs food of flavor and eye appeal.

Seal all packages tightly, too. Air seeps in through even the tiniest openings.

What about the shrink-film wrap on meats in self-serve counters? It breathes so it is unsuitable for freezer storage beyond 2 weeks. Overwrap these packages with one of the moisture/vapor-proof materials.

PILAF

½ cup fine noodles, broken in pieces
2 tablespoons butter or margarine
1 can (10¾ ounces) condensed chicken broth
⅓ cup water
½ cup raw regular rice

In saucepan, brown noodles in butter; stir often. Add remaining ingredients. Bring to a boil; reduce heat. Cover; cook over low heat 20 minutes or until liquid is absorbed. Stir occasionally. Makes about 2 cups.

MORNAY SAUCE

1 can (10¾ ounces) condensed cream of mushroom soup
½ cup shredded natural Swiss cheese
⅓ cup light cream or milk
2 tablespoons grated Parmesan cheese

In saucepan, combine ingredients. Heat until cheese melts; stir often. Serve over cooked meats, poultry, fish, vegetables, or poached eggs. Makes about 1½ cups.

TOMATO SOUP CAKE

2¼ cups cake flour or 2 cups all-purpose flour
1⅓ cups sugar
4 teaspoons baking powder
1 teaspoon baking soda
1½ teaspoons allspice
1 teaspoon cinnamon
½ teaspoon ground cloves
1 can (10¾ ounces) condensed tomato soup
½ cup hydrogenated shortening
2 eggs
¼ cup water

Preheat oven to 350°F. Generously grease and flour two round layer pans, 8 or 9″ or an oblong pan, (13x9x2″). Measure dry ingredients into large bowl. Add soup and shortening. Beat at low to medium speed for 2 minutes (300 strokes with a spoon) scraping sides and bottom of bowl constantly. Add eggs and water. Beat 2 minutes more, scraping bowl frequently. Pour into pans. Bake 35 to 40 minutes. Let stand in pans 10 minutes; remove and cool on rack. Frost with your favorite white frosting. For a 9″ tube pan, bake 1 hour.

Nut or Raisin: After mixing, fold in 1 cup chopped nuts or 1 cup raisins. Bake 35 to 40 minutes.

Date and Nut: After mixing, fold in 1 cup chopped walnuts and 1 cup chopped dates. (Use 1 to 2 tablespoons flour to sprinkle over dates while chopping them.) Bake in 9″ layers or 13x9x2″ pan for 40 to 45 minutes.

ALL 'ROUND BARBECUE SAUCE

1 can (10¾ ounces) condensed tomato soup
2 to 4 tablespoons sweet pickle relish
¼ cup finely chopped onion
1 tablespoon brown sugar
1 tablespoon vinegar
1 tablespoon Worcestershire

In saucepan, combine ingredients. Cover; cook over low heat 10 minutes. Stir occasionally. Use as a barbecue sauce for chicken, frankfurters, hamburgers, or steak. Makes about 1½ cups.

MINI-PIZZAS

1 can (11 ounces) condensed tomato bisque soup
1 small clove garlic, minced
1 teaspoon oregano leaves, crushed
4 English muffins or hamburger buns, split and toasted
1 cup shredded Mozzarella cheese

In saucepan, combine soup, garlic, and oregano. Heat; stir occasionally. Spread soup mixture on muffins; top with cheese. Broil 4 inches from heat until cheese melts. Makes 8 mini-pizzas.

BEEFY BITE-SIZE NIBBLERS

1 pound ground beef
¼ cup finely chopped celery
¼ cup finely chopped onion
1 can (10¾ ounces) condensed cream of mushroom soup
2 tablespoons prepared barbecue sauce
2 packages (about 8 ounces each) refrigerated crescent dinner rolls
¼ cup water
½ teaspoon chili powder

In skillet, brown beef and cook celery and onion until tender (use shortening if necessary); stir to separate meat. Pour off fat. Stir in ¼ cup soup and barbecue sauce. Meanwhile, on lightly floured board, roll each package of rolls into a 12-inch square. Cut each square into 16 (3x3″) pieces. Place about 1 tablespoon of ground beef mixture on each square. Roll up; seal ends. Bake at 450°F. for 8 minutes or until brown. Serve hot. In saucepan, combine remaining soup, water, and chili powder. Heat a few minutes to blend flavors. Serve as a dip with roll-ups. Makes 32 appetizers.

GAZPACHO

- **1 can (10¾ ounces) condensed tomato soup**
- **1 cup water**
- **1 tablespoon olive oil**
- **2 tablespoons wine vinegar**
- **1 large clove garlic, minced**
- **1 cup chopped cucumber**
- **½ cup chopped green pepper**
- **¼ cup chopped onion**

Combine soup, water, oil, vinegar, and garlic. Chill 4 hours or more. Serve in chilled bowls. Pass chilled vegetables for garnish. Makes about 2 cups.

Blender Version: Reduce to ½ cup chopped cucumber, ¼ cup chopped green pepper, and 2 tablespoons chopped onion. In blender, combine all ingredients and 1 slice toast. Blend until smooth. Chill 4 hours or more. Serve in chilled bowls. Pass additional chilled vegetables for garnish. Makes about 3 cups.

MARINATED VEGETABLE SALAD

- **1 can (10¾ ounces) condensed chicken broth**
- **4 medium carrots (about ½ pound), sliced**
- **2 cups cauliflowerets**
- **2 small zucchini (about ½ pound), diagonally sliced**
- **1 cup (about ¼ pound) sliced mushrooms**
- **¼ cup wine vinegar**
- **1 envelope (about 0.6 ounce) Italian dressing mix**

In saucepan, bring broth to boil. Add carrots; simmer 2 minutes. Cool. Stir in remaining ingredients. Chill 4 hours or more. Makes about 7 cups.

COLD CASH: *If you have adequate freezer space, buy perishable specials in large quantities and use when needed. Be sure to rotate your stock, using the oldest items first.*

CHEAPER BY THE OVENFUL: *To get the most cooking done for your money, use your oven to capacity whenever you turn it on. Plan several oven dishes for one meal—baked potatoes and muffins with a casserole, for instance.*

SPREAD-a-BURGER

1 can (10¾ ounces) condensed tomato soup
1 tablespoon prepared mustard
1 tablespoon Worcestershire
1 teaspoon prepared horseradish
1½ pounds ground beef
⅓ cup finely chopped onion
1 teaspoon salt
Generous dash pepper
6 long hard rolls or frankfurter buns, slit and lightly toasted
Sliced process cheese

Combine soup, mustard, Worcestershire, and horseradish. Mix *thoroughly* ⅓ cup soup mixture, beef, onion, salt, and pepper. Spread evenly on buns; *cover edges completely.* Bake at 400°F. for 10 minutes. Top with remaining soup mixture and cheese; bake 5 minutes more. Makes 6 sandwiches.

GERMAN POTATO SALAD

4 slices bacon
¾ cup chopped onion
1 can (10¾ ounces) condensed cream of chicken soup
¼ cup water
2 to 3 tablespoons vinegar
½ teaspoon sugar
⅛ teaspoon pepper
4 cups sliced cooked potatoes
¼ cup chopped parsley

In skillet, cook bacon until crisp; remove and crumble. Cook onion in drippings until tender. Blend in soup, water, vinegar, sugar, and pepper. Add potatoes, parsley, and bacon. Heat; stir occasionally. Makes about 4 cups.

the meaning of metric

It's a fact: The National Bureau of Standards has recommended to Congress that it is in the best interest of the United States to adopt the metric system of measurement. Used by most other countries, metric is simpler than our present system. Conversion will be carried out gradually over a 10-year period, giving everyone plenty of time to adjust.

What does this mean to you? First, it means that the food you buy will be marked in grams and kilograms of weight instead of ounces and pounds. Or in liters in place of pints, quarts, and gallons.

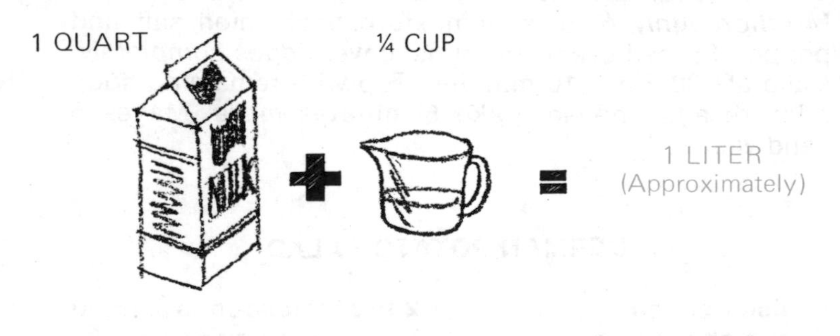

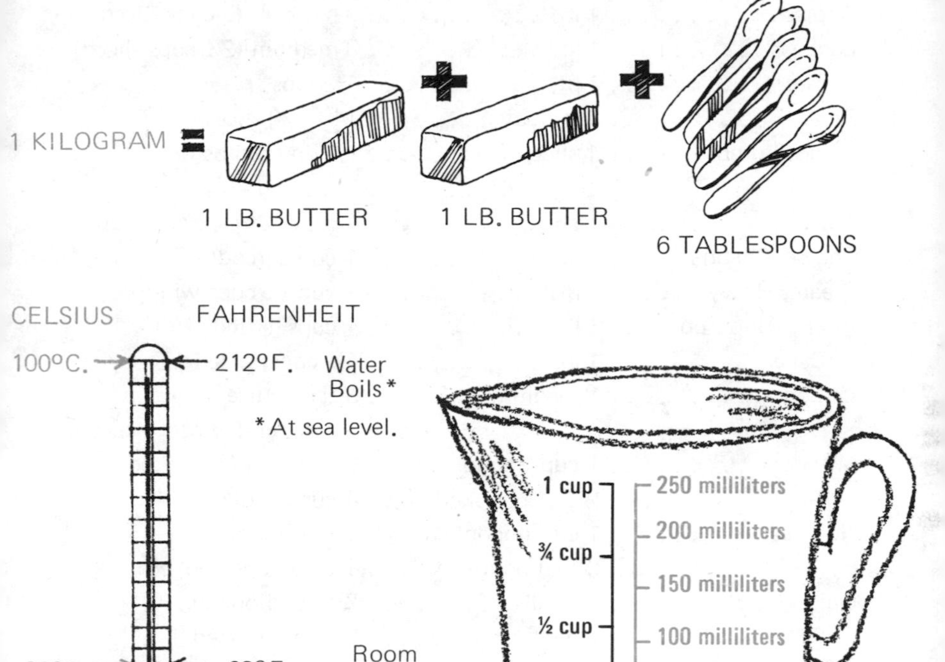

Kitchen measuring utensils will give readings in liters and milliliters rather than teaspoons, tablespoons, cups, pints, quarts, and gallons.

Baking pans will be sized in centimeters instead of inches. Oven, refrigerator, and freezer temperatures will measure Degrees Celsius in place of Degrees Fahrenheit.

Eventually, new recipes will be published which reflect these changes. What will happen to your old favorite recipes? You'll keep on making them the tried and true way, since there's room in every kitchen for two sets of measurers.

everyday equivalents

Item	Amount	Equivalent
Apples	1 lb.	3 medium (3 cups sliced)
Bananas	1 lb.	3 medium (2½ cups sliced)
Berries	1 pt.	1¾ cups
Bread	1 lb. loaf	14 to 20 slices
Bread Crumbs	1 slice bread,	⅓ cup crumbs or
	dry or soft	¾ cup cubes
Butter	1 stick	4 oz. or 8 tbsp. or ½ cup
Cheese, Cheddar	¼ lb.	1 cup shredded
Cream, Heavy	½ pt.	1 cup (2 cups whipped)
Flour, All-purpose	1 lb.	4 cups, sifted
Cake	1 lb.	4½ cups, sifted
Lemon	1 medium	3 tbsp. juice
		1 tbsp. grated peel
Macaroni	1 cup uncooked	2 to 2¼ cups cooked
	½ lb. uncooked	4 cups cooked
Noodles	1 cup uncooked	1¾ cups cooked
	½ lb. uncooked	4 to 5 cups cooked
Onion	1 small	¼ cup chopped
	1 medium	½ cup chopped
	1 large	1 cup chopped
Orange	1 medium	⅓ to ½ cup juice
		2 tbsp. grated peel
Potatoes, White	1 lb.	3 medium
		2⅓ to 2½ cups sliced
		2 cups mashed
Sweet	1 lb.	3 medium
		2½ to 3 cups sliced
Rice, Regular	1 lb.	2½ cups uncooked
		8 cups cooked
Sugar, Granulated	1 lb.	2¼ to 2½ cups
Brown	1 lb.	2¼ cups packed
Confectioners'	1 lb.	4 to 4½ cups unsifted
		4½ to 5 cups sifted
Tomatoes	1 lb.	3 medium

in-a-pinch substitutions

1 tablespoon cornstarch (for thickening)	2 tablespoons flour (approximately)
1 cup fresh whole milk	½ cup evaporated milk plus ½ cup water OR 1 cup reconstituted nonfat dry milk plus 2 tablespoons butter
1 cup sour milk or buttermilk	1 tablespoon lemon juice or vinegar plus enough whole milk to make 1 cup
1 square unsweetened chocolate (1 oz.)	3 tablespoons cocoa plus 1 tablespoon fat
1 cup honey	1¼ cups sugar plus ¼ cup liquid
1 tablespoon fresh herbs	1 teaspoon crumbled dry herbs
1 pound fresh mushrooms	6 ounces canned
1 cup canned tomatoes	approximately 1⅓ cups cut-up fresh tomatoes, simmered 10 minutes

this = that

1 gallon = 4 quarts = 8 pints = 16 cups = 128 ounces or 8 pounds
1 quart = 2 pints = 4 cups = 32 ounces or 2 pounds
1 pint = 2 cups = 16 ounces or 1 pound
1 cup = 8 ounces or ½ pound

☆ ☆ ☆ ☆ ☆

1 cup = 16 tablespoons
½ cup = 8 tablespoons
⅓ cup = 5 tablespoons + 1 teaspoon
¼ cup = 4 tablespoons
⅛ cup = 2 tablespoons

☆ ☆ ☆ ☆ ☆

2 tablespoons = 1 ounce
1 tablespoon = 3 teaspoons

household hints

WHAT A DIFFERENCE A DAY MAKES: *— in the price of bread, at any rate. Watch for day-old specials and stock up the freezer.*

THE BIGGER THE CHEAPER, USUALLY: *Food in large containers generally costs less per ounce, pound, or pint than the same thing in smaller packages. But bigger is better only IF you use the contents often or in large quantities.*

A GOOD EGG: *Store eggs unwashed to protect the coating which keeps them fresh.*

DIVIDE AND CONQUER: *By dividing an electric skillet with foil inserts, you can prepare several small dishes at the same time and save electricity to boot.*

JACK FROST IN VEGETABLE LAND: *Large bags of frozen vegetables usually cost less per ounce than small-sized packages. Pour out just the amount you need and return the rest to the freezer.*

THE TELLTALE TOTAL: *Take along a purse-sized adder to total your purchases as you select them at the market. If the total nears your spending limit, check the foods on your list—as well as those already in the shopping cart—to see what unnecessary items you can omit.*

HOW SWEET IT IS: *There are many tasty uses for the syrup that you drain from canned or frozen fruits. Here are four:*

- *When making gelatin salads or desserts, replace part of the water with syrup.*
- *Combine syrup with mayonnaise, and presto—the perfect dressing for fruit salad.*
- *Thicken syrup with cornstarch for meat glazes or dessert sauces.*
- *Flavor milk or fruit drinks with syrup.*

THE NOTHING-A-DAY POLICY OF CONTAINMENT: *Hold on to those reusable containers (with lids) and use them to store everything from mushrooms to minestrone in refrigerator or freezer. Saves a bundle on throw-away wrapping material.*

WHICH CUPBOARD, MOTHER HUBBARD? *There are some kitchen cabinets that should be bare—of food anyway. Those over the range, near the dishwasher, or by the refrigerator exhaust are too warm for food. Store dishes or pans in these places and save the cooler spots for canned goods and staples to insure longer shelf life.*

LOOK FOR THE SILVER LINING: *But not in your oven. Aluminum foil-lined ovens are less efficient, more costly to operate.*

HOW LOW CAN YOU GO? *Try 25°F. That's the amount to lower your oven setting every time you use glass or ceramic utensils, since these materials transfer heat better than metal.*

JUST AN OLD SOFTY: *To keep brown sugar soft, put it in a plastic bag or a jar with a tight lid, and slip in an apple slice for good measure. Check every so often to see that the slice has not dried out.*

SWEET SOMETHINGS: *If you like the taste of sweet potatoes, do not refrigerate. Temperatures below 50°F. cause starch changes which alter the flavor. This high-in-vitamin A vegetable keeps best in a cool, dark place.*

I'D RATHER CUT IT MYSELF! *Whole chickens are usually cheaper than chicken parts, so being your own butcher is just a matter of* common cents. *For an even bigger budget bonus, buy several whole chickens at sale time, cut them up, then freeze packages of breasts, legs, etc. for up to 10 months.*

PARSLEY, SAGE, ROSEMARY, AND THYME: *There is nothing like an herb—or a subtle combination of them—to take an everyday dish* out of this world *for practically nothing. Become familiar with herbs. Buy them dried or fresh, or better yet, grow your own.*

Fresh herbs do boast the best flavor, but caution—they are usually stronger.

index

Cactus Corn—recipe page 107
Tomato French Dressing—recipe page 114
Mexicali Tacos—recipe page 109

Cheesecake Pie—recipe page 110
Dill-Spiked Onion Rolls—recipe page 111
Chili Shrimp Dip—recipe page 107